WHO WE ARE

WHO WE ARE

THE SOCIAL WORK LABOR FORCE AS REFLECTED IN THE NASW MEMBERSHIP

Margaret Gibelman
Philip H. Schervish

NASW PRESS

NATIONAL ASSOCIATION OF SOCIAL WORKERS
Washington, DC

Barbara W. White, PhD, ACSW, *President*
Sheldon R. Goldstein, ACSW, LISW, *Executive Director*

Library of Congress Cataloging-in-Publication Data

Gibelman, Margaret.
    Who we are : the social work labor force as reflected in the NASW membership / Margaret Gibelman, Philip Schervish.
        p.   cm.
    Includes bibliographical references and index.
    ISBN 0-87101-225-1 (pbk.)
    1. Social workers -- United States. 2. National Association of Social Workers. I. Schervish, Philip H. II. Title.
HV40.8.U6G53   1993
331.7'613613' 0973 -- dc20   93-20452
                                                        CIP

Printed in the United States of America

Cover and interior design by Naylor Design, Inc.

CONTENTS

—

FIGURES

TABLES

—

FOREWORD

From its inception, the profession of social work has been subjected to forces that have questioned its identity and challenged its ability to define its proper place in the configuration of human services professions. Although certainly not unique in this respect, social work is particularly vulnerable to the ebb and flow of public sentiment about the importance of the people it serves, the problems with which it deals, and its entitlement to the resources society will set aside to deal with those problems. As the profession copes with these challenges, there is a growing recognition of the need for information about who we are, what we do, and where we work.

In this book, Margaret Gibelman and Philip Schervish have taken a giant step toward filling this need. Using the 1991 NASW membership data as the basis for their analysis, they have constructed a picture of this segment of the social work labor force. The initial portion of the book acquaints the reader with the characteristics of the database and its strengths and limitations and compares it to what we know about the larger population of nonmember social workers. At this point, the careful scholarship used by the authors is immediately apparent. The chapters that follow take the reader through a logical sequence of descriptive material—the demography of the members, the practice settings in which members are found, the areas of practice and work functions they perform, and what they earn in return for these activities. In each section, the tabular material is enhanced by a clear narrative.

There is a tendency among service-oriented professionals to view labor force statistics as simply an exercise in arithmetic—a dry compilation of their numbers that are of little interest to them and, at best, of marginal use to their profession. This is certainly not true of the material presented in this book. First of all, this compilation is far

from dry. Furthermore, as the authors clearly illustrate in their intro-
ductory comments, these data have many practical uses for policymakers, employers, educators, and researchers, as well as the
NASW staff charged with making programming decisions.

An old proverb states that "the last thing the fish is aware of is the
water in which it swims." With this simple act of describing the
NASW members, Gibelman and Schervish have provided us with a
long-overdue glimpse of the water in which we swim. This book is an
important contribution to the social work literature.

Robert J. Teare, PhD
Professor of Social Work
University of Alabama
Tuscaloosa

PREFACE

Among the purposes of the National Association of Social Workers (NASW), the largest organization of professional social workers in the world, is "to assume responsibility for man- and woman-power planning and development for the range of personnel—professional, technical, and supporting—needed in the provision of social services." The professional labor force is the vehicle through which social work can

- ensure the quality and effectiveness of social work practice in the United States through services to individuals, groups, and communities
- improve the conditions of life in this democratic society
- work in unity to maintain and promote high standards of practice and of preparation for practice toward alleviating or preventing sources of deprivation, distress, and strain (*Bylaws of the National Association of Social Workers,* as amended, 1990).

The achievement of these aims is predicated on the existence of a professional labor force to carry out the profession's mission. Relatively little attention, however, has been paid to the composition of this labor force. Knowledge about "who we are" enables us to assess the characteristics of our labor force against our mandate. Furthermore, this information allows for the exploration of where we are going. Addressing both questions is critical to the continued growth and development of any profession. This book provides answers to the first question in relation to a large subset of the social work population, the NASW membership, and sets forth a beginning agenda by which to identify and debate not only where the profession is headed, but also the extent to which current and future directions are consistent with a consensus definition of where the profession *should* be headed.

We first became interested in the topic of the social work labor force when we began to notice changes in the composition of the social work student body—it was becoming younger, there were fewer males and minorities, and there was a primary interest in clinical practice and intentions to enter independent social work practice. The shift, in our experience, was gradual but distinct. Were we seeing a phenomenon unique only to one geographic area, or was this evidence of larger trends within the current and future professional labor force?

Between 1983 and 1985, NASW and the Council on Social Work Education (CSWE) collaborated on a project, partially funded by the Department of Health and Human Services, to study, debate, and develop recommendations about the development of the social work labor force to meet current and anticipated individual and social needs. One of the authors of this volume participated on that task force. In the course of its deliberations, the joint task force also considered how a database on the social work labor force could be used as a basis for formulating labor force development strategies. The intent was to draw implications, among others, for standards setting, competence certification, and adaptations within social work education curricula to ensure the existence of a professional labor force equipped with the requisite knowledge and skills to respond and lead in meeting future human services needs. A fundamental premise was that the professional labor force should and must evolve within the context of a changing society and emerging social needs.

The recommendations emanating from the June 7–8, 1985, conference on, "The Future of Human Services: Personnel and Practice" provided a working agenda for policy-making bodies, social work education, the social work profession, and other providers of human services. Unfortunately, the pressures of time and changing priorities have left the agenda addressed in only piecemeal fashion. It is our hope that this volume, answering with some degree of clarity who we are, will rekindle the debate about the nature of the professional labor force—what it is and what it should be.

Appreciation is extended to Myles Johnson, formerly of the NASW staff; Sheldon Siegel, dean, Indiana University School of Social Work; and Joseph L. Vigilante, university professor of social policy, Adelphi University, for their enthusiastic participation in the earlier NASW–CSWE effort and their leadership in envisioning a professional labor force that both leads and responds to a changing society.

Special appreciation goes to Ruth Becker, who sent us, from her personal records, the first *Study of Salaries of NASW Members*, which she authored in 1961 during her tenure as NASW Controller. A family friend of the Gibelmans for half a century, Ruth Becker continues to generate ideas about the development of the profession (and of at least one social worker in particular).

No undertaking of this type is accomplished alone. First, acknowledgment and thanks are extended to the thousands of NASW members who, each year, take the time to update the demographic data questions on their membership renewal forms. The data reported herein are accurate in the aggregate only to the extent that members take the extra few minutes to update their records.

We would also like to acknowledge the work of Linda Beebe and Leila Whiting and their staffs in identifying the need for this study, convincing others within NASW of the priority to be afforded this effort, providing access to the data, and providing encouragement and assistance from beginning to end. Their careful reading of the drafts and intellectual contributions are very much appreciated. Sheldon Goldstein and other NASW executive staff have also shown enthusiastic willingness to seriously address the questions raised from this study, ranging from internal data collection procedures to defining a long-range agenda for the association. Fran Pflieger provided able and thoughtful editorial assistance.

Bob Teare, University of Alabama, and Brad Sheafor, Colorado State University, shared with us their work on job analysis, which we have referenced within this volume. It provides an essential groundwork for identifying the functions social workers actually perform. Finally, a special thank-you goes to Peg, Anice, and Katie Schervish for their support and encouragement.

CHAPTER 1

THE EVOLVING SOCIAL WORK LABOR FORCE

—

The average NASW member received a master's degree in social
work sometime during the past nine years, earns $7,350 a year, and
is a caseworker in a federal, state, or municipal governmental agency.
(Becker, 1961, p. 2)

These were among the findings of the National Association of Social
Workers' (NASW's) first survey of members' salaries and employment.
Much has changed since 1961, but NASW's interest in periodically
reviewing and reporting on the demographic composition of its membership has remained consistent. The results of the 1961 study provide
a historical perspective by which to contrast the most recent analysis
(1991) of data on NASW's membership.

This volume reports on the characteristics of social workers who are
members of NASW. Membership in NASW is voluntary, and thus the
sample is self-selected. The information was drawn from the self-
reports of NASW members who completed demographic profiles as
part of their application to join the association and updated the same
information each year on their membership renewal form.

The first report of the salaries and characteristics of NASW members was completed in 1961 (Becker, 1961). Reference to a 1982 report, using 1982 information, appeared in an article detailing shifts in
practice published in the *NASW News* (Staff, 1983, pp. 6–7).

NASW's 1987 salary study (Staff, 1987) included information on
the then-current salaries and employment characteristics of NASW
members in an effort to "examine how these salaries compare with
those paid to the members of other selected professions" (p. 1). The
report was the first effort to build a database on social work practice
and salaries; to publish reports needed by practitioners, administra-

tors, and educators; and to provide a base for periodically updating recommendations about minimum annual salaries. The computerization of the membership records made such comprehensive studies possible.

Unfortunately, the 1987 report provides only a partial base for later comparative analyses, because the profile questions completed by members failed to distinguish between those employed full- and part time. This weakness in the data-collection form was rectified, and beginning with the 1988 membership year, comparative analyses became possible. However, the 1961, 1982, and 1987 reports are an informative and useful source of comparative information, even if they are not completely precise. Data from the Bureau of Labor Statistics (BLS), U.S. Department of Labor, are also reported, when applicable, to compare the characteristics of NASW members with the demographics of the larger labor force in social welfare.

PURPOSES AND USES OF THIS VOLUME

Several questions are consistently posed by policymakers; representatives of federal agencies; administrators of social services and mental health agencies; social work educators; individual social workers, including NASW members; and the association:

- What are the characteristics of professional social workers who are members of NASW?
- How have such characteristics changed over time?
- Where do NASW members work, and what functions do they perform?
- How much money do they earn?
- What factors affect their earning capacity?
- How do the demographics of the membership reflect the changing nature of the social work profession and social work practice?

Answers to these questions allow for an increased understanding of the composition and characteristics of the large proportion of the social work labor force who are members of NASW. They also establish a base for formulating some key policy issues for professional debate. These issues include a consideration of what NASW members do (the functions they perform) versus what the profession and NASW believe and advocate that they do and should be doing; how the practice set-

2

tings and auspices in which NASW members work and the functions performed by them fit with conventional wisdom about these aspects of social work practice; and how NASW's priorities, standards, objectives, and programs relate to and reflect the demographic realities of the association's membership.

Many audiences will find this information useful. *Planners and policy makers* can apply the findings to verify or debate assumptions about the social work labor force and to identify new policy and practice issues for the profession. *Researchers* can compare the findings with data available about other professions and with statistics on social work education to identify key variables that affect recruitment and retention not only in NASW, but in the social work profession. *Social work educators* will find the data valuable in discussions of the reform of curricula and the development of courses. *Boards of directors and administrators* of social welfare organizations and agencies can use this information to inform deliberations on personnel management, recruitment, retention, and compensation. *Individual social workers* can use it to reexamine their own career development and future plans in relation to both other practitioners and professional standards. Finally, comparative salary data (chapter 6) provide a practical framework for negotiating individual and group employment contracts.

Although this volume cites some of the professional literature produced by NASW and other sources, the purpose of such references is to highlight consistencies and disparities among past research, conventional professional theory and wisdom, and statistical findings regarding the demographics and characteristics of NASW members in 1991. Therefore, no attempt was made to conduct an extensive literature search. Rather, the goal was to present findings based on the self-reports of NASW members that expand knowledge of the characteristics of this group of social workers.

NASW MEMBERS IN RELATION TO ALL SOCIAL WORKERS

The NASW bylaws (amended, August 1990), Article IV, detail three classes of membership—regular, associate, and student—and allow additional classes to be established by the Delegate Assembly.

Regular membership is open and limited to anyone who has received an undergraduate or graduate degree from a program accredited or recognized by the Council on Social Work Education (CSWE). *Associate membership* is limited to those who are employed in a social

3

work capacity as determined by the Board of Directors (excluding self-employed practitioners or those in a private group practice) who have an accredited baccalaureate degree in a field other than social work; there are some limitations on membership privileges afforded to associate members. *Student membership* is open to students currently enrolled in a CSWE-accredited social work degree program or a program approved for candidacy; the dues rate for student members is less than that for regular or associate members.

In keeping with the provisions of the bylaws, an additional membership category appears on the NASW membership application form. The category of retired, unemployed, and doctoral candidate membership is open to individuals who are eligible for regular membership and are retired or unemployed and are unsalaried in any field and to doctoral candidates in social work education programs; this group also pays a reduced dues rate.

Although NASW is the largest organization of professional social workers, its membership constitutes an undetermined proportion of the total social work population in the United States who meet the criteria for eligibility but do not join. The BLS (1991) estimated that the total social work labor force was 603,000 in 1991.

Unfortunately, few studies have investigated why some professional social workers choose to join NASW and others do not (Westat, 1984). The authors speculate that social workers may not join for the following reasons:

- financial considerations
- the cost versus the perceived benefits of affiliation
- identification with other primary reference groups
- lack of socialization to membership as part of a social work education program
- lack of information about NASW and its membership benefits
- lack of interest in affiliation with membership organizations
- disagreement with the purposes or programs of NASW.

Characteristics of NASW Members, Lapsed Members, and Nonmembers

Westat, under contract to NASW, conducted a study of the attitudes of 1,205 NASW members, lapsed members, and nonmembers in 1984. The objectives of the study included

- evaluating member, lapsed member, and nonmember perceptions of NASW's current program and service mix
- analyzing lapsed member characteristics and expectations related to their dropping membership and the potential decision to reinstate their membership
- analyzing nonmember characteristics and expectations related to their decision to join professional associations like NASW (Westat, 1984, p. 1-1).

Prequalifying sampling questions identified 22 percent of a random sample of lapsed members who indicated that they were now employed in a field unrelated to social work.

As Table 1.1 shows, the differences in the characteristics of the three groups were as follows:

- A higher proportion of NASW members than of lapsed members and nonmembers were employed in the mental health field.
- A higher proportion of nonmembers than of members or lapsed members were employed in the fields of corrections and public welfare.
- A higher proportion of lapsed members and nonmembers than of members were governmental employees, and proportionally fewer social workers in these two groups worked in the private for-profit sector.

The Westat report (1984, pp. 3-2; 4-1, 4-2) also concluded that NASW members, but not lapsed members and nonmembers, were likely to belong to more than one professional association.

Context of Social Work Practice

The sociopolitical and economic environment has always influenced the goals, priorities, targets of intervention, technologies, and methods of the social work profession (Schneiderman, 1983). The interaction is two-sided, however. The mission of the profession, the motivations and characteristics of the social work labor force, and changes in methods and technology also expand or contract social work's boundaries.

Thus, changes in the profession can originate internally or externally (Walz & Groze, 1991). The role and function of social workers, for example, are affected by both the larger environmental context in which the profession functions (the economy, social need, culture,

TABLE 1.1

Setting and Employment Sector of NASW Members, Lapsed Members, and Nonmembers Surveyed by Westat, 1984 (percentage)

Setting and Employment Sector	Members	Lapsed Members	Nonmembers
Setting			
Business and industry	1	2	1
Corrections	1	2	11
Health	15	15	17
Mental health	38	30	23
Mental retardation	3	5	2
Public welfare	5	12	19
Schools	8	7	9
Social policy	1	3	4
Other	24	15	23
Not stated	2	10	2
Employment Sector			
Government	34	42	49
Private not-for-profit	42	40	39
Private for-profit	19	13	10
Unemployed	2	0	2
Not stated	3	6	1
Base	700	335	170

Note: The percentages do not always total 100 because of rounding.

Source: Westat. (1984). *A study of attitudes of NASW members, lapsed members and non-members*. Rockville, MD: Author.

political preferences, and so on) and the stage of development of professional thought, leadership direction, technology, and mission and goals. In fact, the multiple missions of the profession and the nature of social work practice encompass this dual focus. As Hopps and Pinderhughes (1987, p. 353) commented: "The uniqueness of the social work approach lies in its expertise in acknowledging the interface between intrapersonal and environmental forces."

The War on Poverty of the 1960s is an example of externally driven change. Although social work theory and practice have always included advocacy, the War on Poverty provided an unprecedented opportunity to recruit into the profession and provide job opportunities for those who wished to practice advocacy as a primary function.

The significant movement in the profession toward the private practice of social work has been explained and justified on the basis of the profession's need to expand its mission to take into account and reflect the realities of economic and social change (Jayaratne, Davis-Sacks, & Chess, 1991; Spaulding, 1991). In reality, social workers' interests in the private practice of social work converged with licensing and vendorship—external variables—to shape the course of the profession. At any time, practitioners' interests are both shaped by and help to shape the future of the profession. The relationship is reciprocal.

There are many assumptions about who social workers are and what they do, and the profession's definition of itself and of the boundaries of social work practice are both fluid. Some of the debates in this regard have been waged since the earliest days of the profession. In the early 1900s, Flexner (1915) questioned whether social work is a profession and Richmond (1917) sought to identify the skills required for work with individuals and families. CSWE's 1959 Curriculum Study (Boehm, 1959, p. 40) pointed to "the lack of a single, widely recognized, or generally accepted statement . . . of the aims and purposes of social work." This landmark study concluded that the core activities of social work have not been authoritatively differentiated. In 1973 NASW sought to explicate levels of practice and to develop a classification structure through the promulgation of *Standards for Social Service Manpower* (NASW, 1973). Refinements of definitions and concepts were incorporated in *Standards for the Classification of Social Work Practice* (NASW, 1981).

Changes in the definition of the profession and the characteristics of professional practice reflect the evolving and dynamic nature of social work. Hopps and Pinderhughes (1987, p. 352) saw such changes as positive: "Because social work continues to be seen as emerging and developing, it is important that the profession constantly defines and clarifies itself over the years."

Definition of Social Work Practice

Virtually all professions include specialties within their professional training and practice. The legal profession, for example, includes members who are specialists in tax, criminal, or family law. Medicine, of course, has a wide range of specialty areas, such as dermatology and psychiatry. Social work is equally complex and broad.

As the profession has evolved, the definitions of the profession and its practice have been subject to periodic debate, reexamination, and change. As a profession that interrelates with and seeks to influence the larger socioeconomic and political environment, it is not surprising that the definition of social work is dynamic, rather than rigid and static.

The intent of NASW's *Standards for the Classification of Social Work Practice* (NASW, 1981, p. 3) was "to identify the specific social work content of social service employment and to provide a basis for differentiating among levels of practice." The document defines social work practice as consisting of

> professionally responsible intervention to (1) enhance the developmental, problem-solving, and coping capacities of people, (2) promote the effective and humane operation of systems that provide resources and services to people, (3) link people with systems that provide them with resources, services, and opportunities, and (4) contribute to the development and improvement of social policy.
>
> The interventions are provided to individuals, families, small groups, organizations, neighborhoods, and communities. They involve the disciplined application of knowledge and skill to a broad range of problems which affect the well-being of people, both directly and indirectly. They are carried out at differentiated levels of knowledge and skill, through an organized network of professional social workers within the boundaries of ethical norms established by the profession and the sanction of society. Within these norms, the interventions may be carried out in cooperation with other helping disciplines and organizations as part of any human service enterprise. (p. 6)

Social workers provide services in a wide variety of settings and at all functional levels of practice. For example, they deliver services in private practice, institutions, hospitals, school systems, clinics or centers, and correctional facilities.

Social workers function in direct service, supervision, management, policy development, research, planning, and education–training capacities. In diverse practice settings, they carry out a series of functions (major groupings of tasks and activities that meet the four practice goals identified in Table 1.2), each of which is composed of a set of distinctive tasks. The relationship between the goals of social work

TABLE 1.2

Summary of Social Work Functions

Goal	Functions
To enhance the problem-solving, coping, and development capacities of people	Assessment Diagnosis Detection–identification Support–assistance Advice–counseling Advocacy–enabling
To link people with systems that provide resources, services, and opportunities	Referral Organizing Mobilization Negotiation Exchange
To promote effective and humane operations of systems	Administration–management Program development Supervision Coordination Consultation Evaluation Staff development
To develop and improve social policy	Policy analysis Planning Policy development Reviewing Policy advocacy

Source: *NASW standards for the classification of social work practice.* (1981). (Policy statement 4, p. 12). Silver Spring, MD: National Association of Social Workers.

practice, the objectives related to the particular goals, and the functions and tasks involved is illustrated in the table.

SOURCE AND CHARACTERISTICS OF THE DATA

The NASW membership application form asks prospective members to provide basic demographic and professional background data, which is entered into the association's data base. Each year, as part of the membership renewal process, members are asked to update the information on file.

Data about the characteristics of NASW members were drawn from the information provided directly by the applicants on the application or renewal forms. They were extracted for analysis on July 1, 1991, and include all members whose status was current on that date. A comparison year, 1988, was chosen to provide a base from which to gather information about recent trends in the demographics of members; it is also the first year in which NASW maintained the complete data set in a format comparable to what is now being used. The proportion of members responding to the annual survey was substantially higher in 1991 than in 1988.

The characteristics included in the analysis were derived from the following data:

Variable	Items
Residence	State and zip code
Highest social work degree held	BSW, MSW, DSW, or PhD
Ethnic group	White, African American, Chicano, Puerto Rican, other Hispanic, Native American, Asian, and other
Auspice of primary job and, as applicable, secondary job	Public service, local, state, or federal; military; private not-for-profit, sectarian and nonsectarian; private for-profit
Setting of primary job and, as applicable, secondary job	Outpatient facility, mental health center, institution (nonhospital), private group practice, self-employed solo, elementary or secondary school system, and so forth
Practice area of primary job and, as applicable, secondary job	Children and youths, family services, group services, mental health, and so on
Job function in primary and, as applicable, secondary employment	Direct service, supervision, management–administration, education–training, research, policy, planning
Salary basis	Full or part time

Variable	Items
Total years of social work experience	Years
Academy of Certified Social Workers (ACSW) status	Yes or no

Another question on the form asks about the first and second NASW field-of-practice commission or method council with which members identify. Responses to this question are not included in the analysis because the overwhelming proportion of the respondents did not answer this question and it is not relevant to understanding the characteristics and practice of NASW members.

All categories of members except associate members (those employed in social work capacities but holding a degree other than social work) are included in the membership profile presented in chapter 2. For the more detailed analyses in later chapters, international, retired–unemployed, and student members are excluded, in the interest of including in the data set only those whose status, positions, and salary are the most comparable. In most analyses, BSW, MSW, and DSW–PhD members are analyzed separately.[1]

Limitations of the Data

The study population is limited to NASW members. The precise number of social workers in the United States is not known, since no census category is specific to this profession or includes the educational requirement of a BSW or MSW from an accredited social work education program. Therefore, information is not available to compare the characteristics of NASW members with the larger population of social workers in the United States. Furthermore, it is not known whether the characteristics of social workers who choose to join or do not choose to join NASW differ.

It is possible, however, to derive some proportional estimates of the NASW membership to the total social welfare labor force. The first NASW demographic study of its membership (Becker, 1961) coincided

---

[1]Social workers may be employed in more than one job and one practice setting. For example, a social worker may work half time for a family service agency and maintain a private clinical practice or be employed by a university to teach mental health practice, but perform consultation or research for another agency or in independent practice. Observations about these combinations are made later in this volume.

with a BLS study (1961) on social welfare personnel. That BLS study included in its analysis selected positions in health, recreation, and welfare agencies. According to Becker (p. 2), "the list of job titles in the BLS study contained positions that would fall within the NASW Working Definition of Social Work Practice as well as those which might not fall within the definition." Furthermore, both persons who were eligible and not eligible for NASW membership were included in the BLS data set.

Using the broader category of social welfare, rather than social work personnel, the BLS definition, exclusive of recreation workers, was estimated to be approximately 105,000 during summer 1960. In March 1961, there were 28,000 NASW members, 22,000 of whom were employed. Thus, Becker (1961, p. 2) estimated that in 1961, 21 percent of all people in the social welfare field were NASW members.

The BLS *Household Data Survey: Employed Civilians by Detailed Occupation, 1983–1991* (BLS, 1991) listed 603,000 social workers (exclusive of recreation and religious workers) out of a total of 1,124,000 social, recreation, and religious workers, whereas the 1991 NASW membership database included 100,899 working members with social work degrees from accredited schools. Thus, in 1991 it was estimated that 16.7 percent of all people in the social welfare field were members of NASW.

In their ongoing study of the National Social Work Task Analysis, Teare and Sheafor (1992) also compared the characteristics of NASW members with a large, composite population of professionally trained social workers. They compiled data from three sources—the ACSW Validation Study (1983–84), the Occupational Social Work Study (1984–85), and the ACBSW Study (1988–90) to derive a composite master data file of social workers.[2] The master data file consists of

---

[2]The sample for the ACSW Validation Study was drawn from the NASW Data Bank and hence totally represents NASW members. Seventy-seven percent (*n* = 5,397) of the composite master data file of 7,000 thus consists of NASW members. The sample for the Occupational Social Work Study was drawn from source lists of occupational social workers (including NASW), the rosters of committees, lists of practitioners and vendors, and the ALMACA membership list. Seven percent (*n* = 499) of the composite master data file thus includes both NASW members and nonmembers. The sample for the ACBSW Validation Study was drawn from 349 accredited BSW programs and NASW-BSW lists. Nineteen percent (*n* = 1,363) of the composite master data file resulting from the ACBSW Validation Study data includes both NASW and non-NASW members.

7,000 individual social workers, some of whom are members of NASW and others who are not. The majority of the those included in the sample, however, are NASW members. Nevertheless, the inclusion of non-NASW members in the composite sample allows for comparisons with the NASW membership (see Table 1.3).

This comparison between a composite group representing NASW and non-NASW members and a group composed exclusively of NASW members suggests that there are differences between social workers who are NASW members and those who are not. For example, the proportions of men and of persons with direct service and management functions in the composite population are significantly higher than the proportions in the NASW membership. The composite group also has fewer years of experience than does the NASW membership. Clearly, an in-depth investigation is needed to determine the characteristics of the entire social work labor force and of the NASW membership.

An additional limitation is the currency of the information on NASW members. Although membership is renewed each year, not all members update their profile information on the application form, and some do not complete all the questions. Therefore, a relatively large proportion of the data are missing. A related problem is that when a member updates only part of his or her profile, information is retained from the member's earlier responses to those questions for which no new responses are provided. Thus, for example, in 1991 a member may have updated information on his or her employment auspice, but not on his or her salary. Therefore, the old salary figure (from the last time the member responded to the salary question) would appear as part of the updated record.

Another limitation is that of terminology. Information is solicited from members about their specialization, field of practice, practice setting, and auspice. These terms may not be commonly understood or defined by NASW members, and no definitions are presented on the application forms. Thus, for example, the respondents may not distinguish accurately between private not-for-profit and private for-profit auspices.

Variations in the number of respondents from question to question suggest that the distinctions among practice area, practice setting, and auspice of practice may not be readily understood and that respondents only answered when they were reasonably sure of the intent of the question. This would account, in part, for variations in the number of responses by item.

TABLE 1.3

Comparison of Composite Data Set and NASW Membership

Item	Composite n^a	Composite $\%^b$	NASW n^a	NASW $\%^b$
Gender				
Male	2,366	30.8	28,952	22.4
Female	4,606	65.8	100,236	77.6
Location				
Northeast	2,264	32.2	38,954	28.8
North Central	2,136	25.6	34,709	25.6
South	1,505	21.5	31,106	23.0
West	1,060	15.1	21,444	15.8
Other	—	—	9,144	6.8
Ethnicity				
African American	537	7.3	6,885	5.8
White	6,361	88.0	103,529	88.0
Hispanic	123	1.7	3,170	2.7
Asian	101	1.4	1,815	1.5
Other	85	1.2	1,580	1.3
Setting				
Social service	2,107	30.1	21,970	15.9
Private practice	472	6.8	15,432	11.2
Membership organization	76	1.3	715	0.5
Hospital	1,354	19.3	18,820	13.7
Institution	266	3.8	2,738	2.0
Outpatient	1,171	16.7	15,310	11.1
Group home	178	2.5	2,311	1.7
Nursing home–hospice	220	3.0	2,343	1.7
Courts–criminal justice system	118	1.7	1,311	0.9
College–university	390	5.6	4,374	3.2
Schools	418	6.0	5,790	4.2
Other	181	2.6	2,095	1.5

continued

TABLE 1.3—Continued

Item	Composite n^a	Composite $\%^b$	NASW n^a	NASW $\%^b$
Practice				
Children/youth	975	13.9	15,753	11.4
Community organization	92	1.3	1,132	0.8
Family service	945	13.5	10,737	7.8
Corrections	110	1.6	1,152	0.8
Group services	30	0.4	461	0.3
Medical–health	920	13.1	11,677	21.9
Mental health	1,703	24.3	30,153	21.9
Public assistance/welfare	128	1.8	871	0.6
School social work	359	5.1	4,429	3.2
Aged service	437	6.2	4,588	3.3
Substance abuse	165	2.4	4,371	3.2
Developmental disabilities	328	4.7	2,651	1.8
Other disabilities	40	0.6	518	0.4
Occupational	69	1.0	716	0.5
Education	277	4.0	—	—
Other	422	6.1	5,413	3.9
Function				
Direct service	4,053	57.9	65,286	47.4
Supervision	640	9.1	5,984	4.3
Management	1,639	23.4	15,739	11.4
Policy, planning, research	83	1.2	3,335	2.4
Consultation	128	1.8	1,589	1.2
Education	420	6.0	4,450	3.2
Non–social work	—	—	2,619	1.9
Experience (average number of years)	12.2	—	19.3	—

Source: Teare, R., & Sheafor, B. (1992, August). *The national social work task force analysis studies* (professional seminar presented to the NASW and CSWE staffs). Washington, DC: Authors.

[a] The total numbers differ in each category because the respondents did not answer all the questions.
[b] The percentages refer to the proportion who responded in each category.

These definitional problems are particularly acute in regard to the question about social work specialties. A majority of the respondents indicated "other social work" or "generic" as their specialty. *Generic* social work may be variously defined, and *casework*, the term used on the specialty question, is no longer commonly used to describe direct practice with individuals and families.

Indeed, the social work vocabulary has changed. In 1961, the term used to describe a social worker engaged in direct practice was *caseworker* and the practice was called *casework*. Now, those engaged in one-to-one interventions with clients are referred to as *clinical social workers* or *clinicians*. Unfortunately, the vocabulary used in the NASW application and renewal forms do not always reflect the shifts in terminology that have occurred in the profession. A revision of the terms used to describe specialties may yield more accurate responses.

Chapter 2 includes information about specialties and ACSW membership that are not reported elsewhere in this volume. The problems with terminology rendered a further analysis of specialties unwarranted. Because of state licensure and newer forms of credentialing in addition to the ACSW, responses to this question provide little insight about the characteristics of NASW members.

Because of the limitations of the data base, information is not available about the precise nature of the work of social workers who are engaged in social work practice. Similarly, it is not possible to report on the characteristics of the clients–patients whom social workers serve. However, the ongoing job analyses of Teare and Sheafor provide an important model for other researchers to use in defining the nature of social work interventions precisely.

Given these limitations, any generalizations to all social workers in the United States must be made with extreme caution.

ANALYSIS OF THE DATA

The NASW membership database included 134,240 members in 1991 and 116,296 in 1988. The entire data set was used to establish a membership profile presented in chapter 2. For analyses in chapters 3 through 5, a subset of the total membership data base was created to represent social workers who are currently employed (full- or part time). Chapter 6, which reports on the salaries of NASW members, includes a subset of employed full-time members—100,899 in 1991 and 86,091 in 1988.

Using the Statistical Package for the Social Sciences, the authors conducted frequencies and cross-tabulations for each variable in the NASW membership application-renewal questionnaire (see the appendix). The results of the frequencies and cross-tabulations were used in the descriptions and accompanying narrative interpretations of NASW members.

REFERENCES

Becker, R. (1961). *Study of salaries of NASW members*. New York: National Association of Social Workers.

Boehm, W. (1959). *Objectives of the social work curriculum of the future, Social Work Curriculum Study, Vol. 1*. New York: Council on Social Work Education.

Bureau of Labor Statistics. (1961). *Salaries and working conditions of social welfare manpower in 1960*. New York: National Social Welfare Assembly.

Bureau of Labor Statistics. (1991). *Household data survey: Employed civilians by detailed occupation, 1983–1991*. Washington, DC: Author.

Flexner, A. (1915). Is social work a profession? In *Proceedings of the National Conference of Charities and Corrections* (pp. 576–590). Chicago: Hildman Printing Co.

Hopps, J., & Pinderhughes, E. (1987). Profession of social work: Contemporary characteristics. In A. Minahan (Ed.-in-Chief), *Encyclopedia of social work* (18th ed., pp. 351–365). Silver Spring, MD: National Association of Social Workers.

Jayaratne, S., Davis-Sacks, M. L., & Chess, W. (1991). Private practice may be good for your health. *Social Work, 36*, 224–232.

National Association of Social Workers. (1973). *Standards for social service manpower*. Silver Spring, MD: Author.

National Association of Social Workers. (1981). *NASW standards for the classification of social work practice* (Policy statement 4). Silver Spring, MD: Author.

National Association of Social Workers. (1990). *Bylaws of the National Association of Social Workers*. Silver Spring, MD: Author.

Richmond, M. (1917). *Social diagnosis*. New York: Russell Sage Foundation.

Schneiderman, L. (1983). The future context of social work practice. Unpublished paper, Commission on Educational Planning, Council on Social Work Education, New York.

Spaulding, E. (1991). *Statistics on social work education in the United States: 1990.* Alexandria, VA: Council on Social Work Education.

Staff. (1983, November). Membership survey shows practice shifts. *NASW News*, pp. 6–7.

Staff. (1987). *Salaries in social work: A summary report on the salaries of NASW members, July 1986–June 1987.* Silver Spring, MD: National Association of Social Workers.

Teare, R., & Sheafor, B. (1992, August). *The national social work task force analysis studies* (professional seminar presented to the NASW and CSWE staffs). Washington, DC: Authors.

Walz, T., & Groze, V. (1991). The mission of social work revisited: An agenda for the 1990s. *Social Work, 36,* 500–504.

Westat. (1984). *A study of attitudes of NASW members, lapsed members and non-members.* Rockville, MD: Author.

CHAPTER 2

DEMOGRAPHIC OVERVIEW OF THE NASW MEMBERSHIP

This chapter presents a profile of all categories of NASW members in 1991 and compares it to the profile of members in 1988. Because this overview includes data on students, findings related to income would be skewed in a negative direction and would not accurately reflect salary ranges. Therefore, data related to income are omitted here. A full discussion of the income of full-time employed NASW members is presented in chapter 6.

NASW MEMBERSHIP

From 1988 to 1991, the NASW membership grew by 15 percent, from 116,296 in 1988 to 134,240 in 1991. These numbers do not reflect the total number of social workers practicing in the United States. According to the BLS (1991), which annually tallies the working population by occupational title, 537,000 employees held the title of social worker in 1988, compared to 603,000 in 1991—a 12 percent increase.[1] The true number of professionally educated social workers in the United States falls somewhere between the two totals. The profession's rate of growth seems to be slightly less than NASW's rate of growth (see Figure 2.1).

---

[1]The BLS regularly collects data on individuals by position title. People in these positions may or may not hold social work degrees or fit the NASW definition of a professional social worker. The BLS (1991) estimated that about 49 percent of those whose positions had social work titles in 1991 had social work degrees at the BSW, MSW, or doctoral level.

FIGURE 2.1

NASW versus BLS Counts of Social Workers: 1988 and 1991

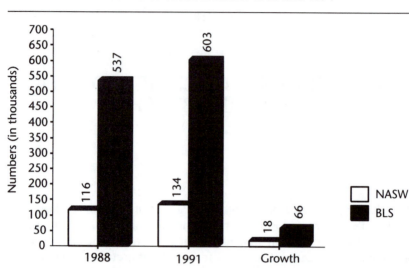

GENDER

The NASW membership is overwhelmingly female. In 1988, 74.9 percent (73,321) of the 97,833 members responding to this question were female and 25.1 percent (24,512) were male. In 1991, of the 125,414 respondents the proportion of women increased to 77.3 percent (96,953), and the proportion of men decreased to 22.7 percent (28,461).

The difference between the genders in the BLS survey was not as great as in the NASW figures. The BLS reported that women constituted 66 percent of the profession in 1988 and 68 percent in 1991 (see Figure 2.2).

ETHNICITY

Data related to the ethnicity of NASW members reveal a consistent pattern in 1988 and 1991. Of the 92,318 who indicated their ethnicity, 88.4 percent (81,632) were white in 1988, compared with 88.1 percent of 113,823 respondents (100,227) in 1991. African Americans were the second largest ethnic group in the membership, at 5.7 percent

FIGURE 2.2

Gender of NASW Members: NASW versus BLS Counts

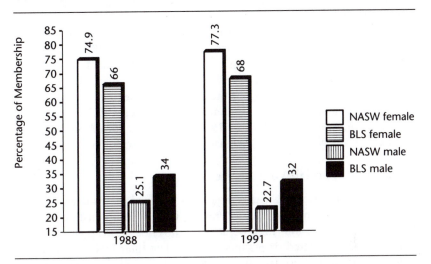

(5,254) in 1988 and 5.9 percent (6,690) in 1991. In both 1988 and 1991, Asians made up 1.5 percent of the membership and Native Americans, 0.5 percent. Hispanics, including Chicanos, Puerto Ricans, and other Hispanics, constituted 2.4 percent (2,206) of the membership in 1988 and 2.6 percent (3,002) in 1991 (see Table 2.1).

TABLE 2.1

Ethnicity of NASW Members

	1988		1991		
Ethnicity	n	%ᵃ	n	%	% Change
White	81,632	88.4	100,227	88.1	−0.3
African American	5,254	5.7	6,690	5.9	0.2
Hispanic	2,206	2.4	3,002	2.6	0.2
Asian	1,427	1.5	1,751	1.5	0.0
Native American	463	0.5	602	0.5	0.0
Other	1,336	1.4	1,551	1.4	0.0
Total respondents	92,318		113,823		

ᵃPercentages do not total 100 because of rounding.

21

EDUCATION

The highest degree of the vast majority of NASW members is the MSW. Out of the 131,924 members who responded, 87.8 percent (115,766) held full membership at the MSW level in 1991. The proportion was the same in 1988, when 87.5 percent (93,979) of the 107,454 who responded to this question reported the MSW as their highest degree (see Table 2.2).

In 1988, 7.8 percent (8,417) of the responding membership consisted of BSW social workers, compared to 7.4 percent (9,799) in 1991. Only 4.7 percent (5,058) of 1988 members reported holding a doctoral degree, with a slight increase to 4.8 percent (6,359) in 1991.

Date of Highest Social Work Degree

The largest proportion of NASW members received their highest social work degree between 1986 and 1990; this finding held constant in 1988 and 1991. In 1988, 22.8 percent (19,601) of the responding members had completed or planned to complete their highest degree between 1986 and 1990. (Because students are included in this overview, the date of the highest social work degree includes the anticipated date for some respondents.) In 1991, 22.5 percent (28,006) of the responding members completed their highest social work degree between 1986 and 1991 (see Figure 2.3).

From 1988 to 1991, there was a discernible pattern in the loss of members who received their highest social work degree in 1980 and earlier. For example, in 1988, the proportion of members with a degree date of 1980 or earlier was 66.9 percent, whereas in 1991, it was 46.8 percent. The proportion of members with a highest degree date of 1961–70 dropped from 19.2 percent in 1988 to 12.4 percent in 1991.

TABLE 2.2

Highest Degree Held by NASW Members

Highest Degree	1988		1991		
	n	%	n	%	% Change
BSW	8,417	7.8	9,799	7.4	–0.4
MSW	93,979	87.5	115,766	87.8	0.3
DSW–PhD	5,058	4.7	6,359	4.8	0.1
Total respondents	107,454		131,924		

FIGURE 2.3

Date of Receipt of the Highest Social Work Degree of NASW Members

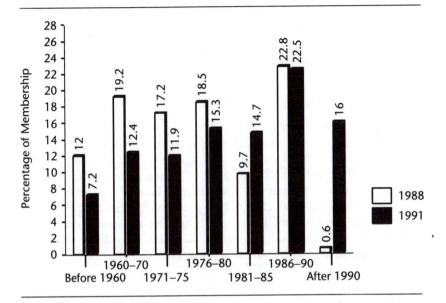

These data may reflect the socioeconomic environment of the times in that the enrollment in schools of social work declined during the late 1970s and early 1980s (CSWE, 1986). These losses were compensated, to some degree, by the increase in enrollments in the late 1980s, as reflected in the number of recent graduates who became NASW members in 1988 (2,792) and 1990 (4,628). Also, there seems to be a delay between the receipt of a degree and membership in NASW.

Nonetheless, the postdegree experience of NASW members is decreasing. In 1991, 92.8 percent (115,410) of the responding members received their highest social work degree after 1961, compared to 88 percent (75,708) of responding members in 1988. By 1991, 53.2 percent of the members earned their highest social work degree after 1981.

AGE

The median age range of NASW members, for both 1988 and 1991, was 41 to 45 years. This figure corresponds with national demographics on the baby-boom generation. Consistent with the findings for the date of

23

receipt of the highest social work degree, the data suggest that the NASW membership is getting younger. In 1988, 8.5 percent (8,852) of the 103,713 responding members were aged 30 or under, compared to 14.6 percent (17,907) of the 122,587 members responding in 1991. Members aged 51 and over decreased in this period, from 28.8 percent (29,871) of the members responding in 1988 to only 23.4 percent (28,707) of those responding in 1991 (see Figure 2.4).

GEOGRAPHIC DISTRIBUTION OF MEMBERS

The geographic distribution of NASW members was compared for the standard regions of the United States used by the U.S. Department of Health and Human Services. The data indicate little change in geographic distribution from 1988 to 1991. The largest geographic distributions of members were in the Mid-Atlantic, East North Central, and South Atlantic regions, which is not surprising since these are the largest U.S. population centers. However, shifts from the North and Northeast to the South and Southwest, consistent with shifts in the general population, also occurred (see Table 2.3).

FIGURE 2.4

Age of NASW Members

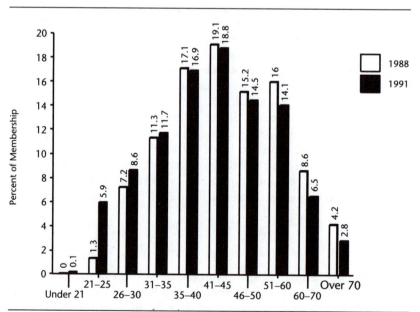

TABLE 2.3

NASW Members by Geographic Distribution

Region	1988 (n = 115,776)	1991[a] (n = 133,739)	% Change
New England	10.5	10.4	−0.1
Mid-Atlantic	23.6	22.9	−0.5
East North Central	19.1	18.8	−0.3
West North Central	6.5	6.5	0.0
South Atlantic	14.0	14.7	+0.7
East South Central	3.0	3.2	+0.2
West South Central	6.5	6.7	+0.2
Mountain	4.3	4.6	+0.3
Pacific	12.4	12.2	−0.2
Territories	0.1	0.1	0.0

[a]Percentages do not total 100 because of rounding.

EXPERIENCE

Approximately 83 percent (111,357) of the 134,240 members responded to the question about experience in 1991, compared to 60 percent (69,358) in 1988. In 1991, the two largest groups of respondents were those with two years of experience, 19.3 percent (21,520), and those with 11 to 15 years of experience, 16 percent (17,776) (see Figure 2.5).

These findings contrast significantly with the 1988 data, when only 1.9 percent (1,315) of the respondents had under two years of experience. NASW's efforts to recruit students and new graduates may account for this dramatic shift.

In 1988, 21.4 percent (14,859) of the respondents had over 26 years of experience, compared to 13.5 percent (15,011) in 1991. The average years of experience reported by the 1988 respondents was 11 to 15 years, compared to 6 to 10 years in 1991. These data, in conjunction with the data on the date of receipt of the highest degree and the age of the members, suggest that there has been a dramatic reversal in the pattern of experience of NASW members, from very experienced in 1988 to much less experienced in 1991 (see Figure 2.6).

This reversal of the pattern is even more evident when the data are combined into two categories—zero to 10 years of experience and 11 or more years of experience. In 1991, 47.6 percent (53,005) of the respondents had zero to 10 years of experience versus 26.1 percent

FIGURE 2.5

Work Experience of NASW Members

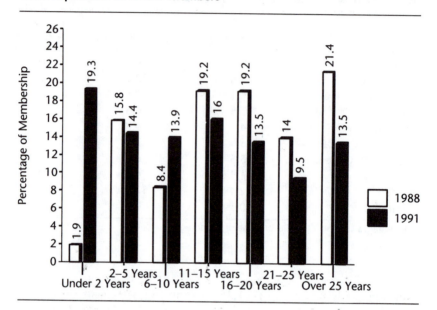

FIGURE 2.6

Work Experience of NASW Members
(collapsed categories)

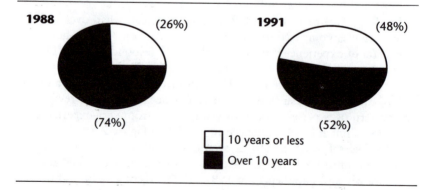

(18,114) in 1988, and 52.4 percent (58,352) had 11 or more years of experience in 1991, compared to 73.9 percent (37,930) in 1988. These shifts are examined in greater detail in chapter 3.

Full- versus Part-time Employment

Of the 67,908 members who responded to the question about full- or part-time employment in 1991, 52,306 (77 percent) indicated that they were employed full time and 15,602 (23 percent) said they were employed part time. Almost 50 percent of the membership did not respond to this question. In 1988, only 15 percent of the members responded with information about full- versus part-time employment; 75 percent (13,231) of them indicated that they were employed full time (see Figure 2.7).

PRACTICE

Areas

In both 1988 and 1991, the top primary practice areas of the members were, in order, mental health, children, medical clinics, and family services (see Table 2.4). The pattern was similar to that of 1988, with consistent rank orders and proportions.

In 1991, 33.1 percent (44,441) of the total data set of 134,240 indi-

FIGURE 2.7

Work Status of NASW Members

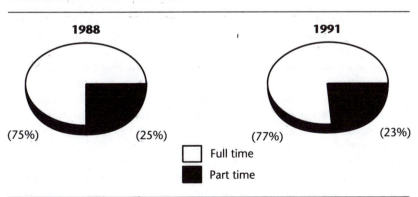

TABLE 2.4

Percentage of NASW Members by Primary and Secondary Practice Areas

Area of Practice	1988 Primary (n = 89,443)	1988 Secondary (n = 35,666)	1991 Primary (n = 107,921)	1991 Secondary (n = 44,441)
Mental health	29.0	25.1	30.5	26.3
Children	17.0	12.0	17.3	12.6
Medical clinics	12.9	5.9	12.2	5.7
Family	12.2	20.6	11.4	19.1
Aged	5.3	6.3	5.1	5.4
Substance abuse	4.1	7.6	4.7	9.7
Schools	4.2	2.2	4.4	2.5
Mental retardation, developmental and physical disabilities	3.7	3.7	3.6	3.6
Corrections	1.5	1.5	1.3	1.6
Community organization– planning	1.6	2.8	1.2	2.2
Public assistance	1.0	0.8	1.0	0.7
Occupational	0.8	1.0	0.8	0.9
Groups	0.6	2.8	0.5	2.9
Other	0.9	1.0	0.2	0.2
Combined	5.2	6.7	5.8	6.6

cated a secondary practice area, compared to 30.7 percent (35,666) of the total data set of 116,296 in 1988. For both years, the vast majority of NASW members (over two-thirds) did not have or failed to indicate that they had a secondary practice area.

The secondary practice areas were, in rank order and proportion, similar to those of the primary practice areas in three of four categories. In 1988, 25.1 percent (8,964) of the 35,666 respondents cited mental health services as their secondary practice area, compared to 26.3 percent (11,686) of 44,433 respondents in 1991, a small proportional growth. The second-ranked category in both 1988 and 1991 was family services, which was the fourth-ranked primary practice area in both years. In 1988, 20.6 percent (7,335) of the respondents cited family services as their secondary practice area, compared to

19.1 percent (8,508) in 1991. Children's services and substance abuse services ranked third and fourth, respectively, in both 1988 and 1991.

Specialty

NASW members listed "generic" as their number-one specialty in both 1988 and 1991: 41.9 percent (47,273) in 1988 versus 41.7 percent (55,367) in 1991. The second-ranked specialty for both 1988 and 1991 was "other social work," noted by 23.2 percent (26,192) of the members in 1988 and 31 percent (41,161) in 1991. Because this is a catch-all category and lacks precise definition, it was not possible to ascertain the specialties with which this large group of members identified. The third-ranked category for both years was casework, but a smaller proportion of members cited that specialty in 1991 than in 1988.

FIGURE 2.8

Specialties of NASW Members

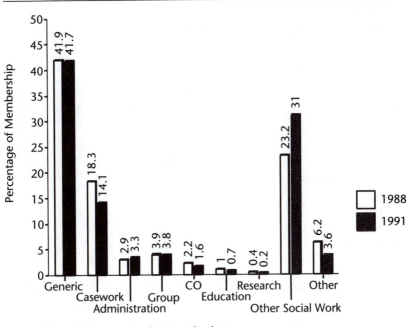

Note: CO = community organization

Settings

In both 1988 and 1991, the rank and proportion of the top four primary practice settings cited by the respondents were virtually identical. In 1988, 26 percent (22,684) of 87,247 respondents declared agencies to be their primary setting of practice, compared to 25 percent (26,568) of 106,194 respondents in 1991. The second-, third-, and fourth-ranked settings were hospitals, medical clinics, and private solo practice, respectively. Private solo practice, as a primary practice setting, increased slightly, from 9.3 percent (8,142) in 1988 to 10.9 percent (11,612) in 1991.

Similarly, the rank and proportion of the top four secondary practice settings for 1988 and 1991 were closely aligned. For both years, the rank order was private solo practice, medical clinic, private group practice, and agency. The proportion of NASW members citing private solo practice increased slightly, from 30.4 percent in 1988 to 31.1 percent in 1991. Other variations were negligible (see Table 2.5).

Universities ranked fifth among the secondary practice settings and

TABLE 2.5

**Percentage of NASW Members by Primary and
Secondary Practice Setting**

Setting	1988		1991	
	Primary ($n = 87,247$)	Secondary ($n = 27,555$)	Primary ($n = 106,194$)	Secondary ($n = 27,555$)
Agency	26.0	10.6	25.0	10.8
Hospital	19.9	7.0	20.0	7.6
Medical clinic	16.2	12.6	16.2	12.9
Private solo practice	9.3	30.4	10.9	31.1
School	5.8	2.5	5.9	2.9
University	4.2	8.2	4.6	8.1
Private group practice	3.8	11.3	4.1	11.6
Group home	2.7	3.3	3.1	3.4
Institution	3.1	2.3	3.0	2.3
Nursing home	2.4	3.6	2.6	3.3
Non–social work setting	2.8	4.8	2.2	3.2
Court	1.5	0.5	1.5	1.9
Membership organizations	0.9	0.3	0.8	1.1

Note: Percentages do not total 100 because of rounding.

sixth among the primary practice settings for both 1988 and 1991. In 1988 and 1991, 8.2 percent (2,269) and 8.1 percent (2,642), respectively, of the members who responded cited them as their secondary practice setting, and 4.6 percent (4,832) and 5.5 percent (4,829), respectively, cited them as their primary practice setting in those years. A larger proportion of NASW members who were affiliated with universities worked part time rather than full time.

Auspices

The four highest-ranked primary auspices under which NASW members were employed remained consistent in 1988 and 1991, although there were some significant proportional shifts (see Table 2.6). For both years, private not-for-profit, private for-profit, public local, and public state auspices were most frequently cited. Of the 87,032 members responding in 1988, 41.6 percent (36,213) noted that their primary auspice was public (federal, state, local, or military), compared to 38.7 percent (39,686) of the 102,617 respondents in 1991. In addition, only a small number of members were employed by the federal government in both years, and the numbers had declined—from 2,933 (3.4 percent) in 1988 to 2,912 (2.8 percent) in 1991.

This downward trend in public auspices was offset by the growth in the proportion of respondents who cited private for-profit as their primary auspice: from 18.5 percent (16,092) in 1988 to 22.2 percent

TABLE 2.6

NASW Members by Primary and Secondary Auspice (percentage)

	1988		1991	
Auspice	Primary (*n* = 87,032)	Secondary (*n* = 21,569)	Primary (*n* = 102,617)	Secondary (*n* = 26,605)
Public local	18.9	10.8	19.2	10.7
Public state	18.5	10.9	15.9	10.4
Public federal	3.4	2.5	2.8	1.9
Public military	0.8	0.9	0.8	0.9
Private not-for-profit sectarian	11.8	8.7	12.4	9.0
Private not-for-profit nonsectarian	28.1	20.8	26.7	20.6
Private for-profit	18.5	45.4	22.2	46.5

(22,769) in 1991. The private not-for-profit sector also showed a decline: from 28.1 percent (24,417) in 1988 to 26.7 percent (27,407) in 1991.

Of the 26,605 NASW members who indicated a secondary auspice in 1991, 12,381 (46.5 percent) identified their auspice as the private for-profit sector. In 1991, the second-ranked auspice was private not-for-profit at 20.6 percent (5,470), followed by public local at 10.7 percent (2,843) and public state at 10.4 percent (2,766).

With regard to the secondary auspice, the same four categories as for the primary auspice ranked highest in 1988, in virtually the same order. From 1988 to 1991, there was a small but discernible increase in the number of members citing private for-profit (both organizational settings and individual–group private practice) as their secondary auspice.

Functions of Members

In both 1988 and 1991, the members who responded overwhelmingly identified direct service as their primary function: 64.1 percent (60,790) of the 94,822 respondents in 1988 and 68 percent (75,083) of the 110,349 respondents in 1991. The second-, third-, and fourth-ranked functions in both years were management, supervision, and education, respectively (see Table 2.7).

TABLE 2.7

Percentage of NASW Members by Primary and Secondary Functions

	1988		1991	
Function	Primary (n = 94,822)	Secondary (n = 42,244)	Primary (n = 110,349)	Secondary (n = 51,418)
Direct service	64.1	32.6	68.0	32.1
Supervision	6.2	17.2	6.2	18.9
Management	16.8	10.2	15.4	10.2
Policy	0.5	2.5	0.5	2.4
Consultant	1.8	14.0	1.5	14.0
Research	0.5	2.2	0.6	2.2
Planning	0.5	2.6	0.4	2.4
Education	5.0	15.5	4.5	15.7
Non–social work	4.5	3.3	2.7	2.1

Note: Percentages do not total 100 because of rounding.

The rankings remained relatively stable for the two years; only the number and proportion of members in direct service and research increased. The number and proportion of members citing all the other primary functions decreased slightly or remained the same.

These data suggest a significant skewing between direct (micro) and indirect (macro) primary functions in social work practice and a small but noticeable decline between 1991 and 1988 in the proportion of members who identified their primary function as macro. For 1991, the policy, consultation, research, and planning functions combined represented only 3,409 of the 110,349 valid responses (3 percent). When management was factored in, the total for macro practice was 18.4 percent (20,444). In 1988, 20.1 percent (19,102) of NASW members listed a macro-level primary function, including management.

A sizable proportion of the members reported that they performed multiple functions in one or more settings. Of the full data set of 134,240 in 1991, 38 percent (51,418) reported a secondary function. Direct service, the largest category, represented 32.1 percent (16,507) of the respondents. In 1988, out of a data set of 116,296, 36 percent (42,244) reported having a secondary function. Of these, 13,770 (32.6 percent) cited direct service as their secondary function.

The proportions and rankings of secondary functions were consistent for 1988 and 1991. Following direct service was supervision, education, consultation, and management, respectively. From 1988 to 1991, there was a small but discernible increase in the proportion of respondents who reported their secondary function as supervision.

ACSW STATUS

In 1988, 50.7 percent (58,987) of the members reported having an active ACSW status, compared to 45.2 percent (60,725) in 1991—a significant decrease. The decrease may be attributed, in part, to the decline in the age, experience, and level and date of the highest social work degree of members between 1988 and 1991.

MEMBERSHIP CATEGORY

In both 1988 and 1991, the vast majority of respondents were full members (see Table 2.8). In both years, 12.8 percent of the membership was composed of students at the PhD–DSW, MSW, or BSW levels; most of the students are studying for their MSWs.

TABLE 2.8

Percentage of NASW Members, by Category of Membership

	1988 (n = 116,296)	1991 (n = 134,240)
PhD–DSW	2.5	2.4
MSW	61.0	60.3
BSW	1.6	2.2
Transitional MSW	7.5	8.1
Transitional BSW	1.5	2.1
Student PhD–DSW	0.8	0.9
Student MSW	9.0	8.5
Student BSW	3.0	3.4
Retired	3.0	2.7
Foreign	0.9	0.4
Other	9.2	9.0

The transitional category comprised 10.2 percent (13,757) of the respondents, up from 9 percent (10,534) in 1988. This category includes social workers who completed their highest degree within the past year and are transferring from BSW or MSW student status to full-member status and receive a discount on the full-membership dues.

CHAPTER HIGHLIGHTS: 1988 TO 1991

- The vast majority of NASW members were women, and the ratio of women to men increased.
- The vast majority of members were white.
- The overwhelming majority of members had MSW degrees.
- Approximately 45 percent of the members were ACSWs in 1991—a significant decrease from 1988.
- Approximately 93 percent of the 1991 members received their highest social work degree after 1961.
- In 1991, the largest proportion of members had under two years of social work experience—a sharp contrast with 1988, when the largest proportion had over 26 years of experience.
- The median age of the members, for both 1988 and 1991, was 41 to 45 years.

- Findings on the date of receipt of the highest social work degree and years of experience indicate that the membership is getting younger.
- Over 75 percent of the members were employed full time.
- Mental health services represented the largest primary practice area, followed, in rank order, by children, medical clinics, and family services.
- Over 30 percent of the members indicated a secondary practice area.
- The four highest-ranked primary practice settings were agencies, hospitals, medical clinics, and private solo practice.
- Private solo practice ranked first as the secondary practice setting.
- Private not-for-profit, private for-profit, public local, and public state were the highest-ranked primary auspices, respectively.
- The number and proportion of members employed under public auspices decreased.
- The number and proportion of members employed under private for-profit auspices increased.
- Relatively few members worked under federal auspices.
- The most frequently reported secondary function was direct practice.
- Approximately 42 percent of the members describe their specialty as generic.

REFERENCES

Bureau of Labor Statistics. (1991). *Household data survey: Employed civilians by detailed occupation, 1983–1991*. Washington, DC: Author.

Council on Social Work Education. (1986). *Statistics on social work education in the United States: 1985*. Washington, DC: Author.

CHAPTER 3

WHO WE ARE

GENDER, AGE, ETHNICITY, EDUCATION, GEOGRAPHIC REPRESENTATION, AND EXPERIENCE

———

This chapter presents findings on the demographics of a subset of NASW members: those who were employed full- or part time in 1988 and 1991. Thus, student, associate, and retired–unemployed members were excluded from the analysis. For 1991, the total population of employed social workers was 100,899; for 1988, it was 86,091. It should be recalled that when they complete the demographic profile each year as part of their membership renewal many members do not respond to all questions. Thus, the number of responses may vary considerably from question to question. Again, data for both 1988 and 1991 are compared to identify discernible trends over time.

GENDER

Of the 86,091 employed NASW members in 1988, 82.7 percent (71,204) responded to the question about gender. In that year, 72.3 percent (51,479) were women and 27.7 percent (19,725) men. In 1991, of the 92.6 percent (93,419) of employed members who responded, 75.7 percent (70,677) were women (see Figure 3.1).

Although the majority of members in all ethnic groups were women in both years, there are some proportional differences among the male members by ethnicity. Proportionately, there were fewer African American male NASW members than male NASW members of other ethnic groups, at 22.2 percent (756) in 1988 and 19.4 percent (908) in 1991. In contrast, there were proportionately more Chicano male members than male members of other ethnic groups, at 39.2 percent (211) in 1988 and 36.3 percent (291) in 1991 (see Table 3.1).

FIGURE 3.1

Gender of Working NASW Members, 1988 and 1991

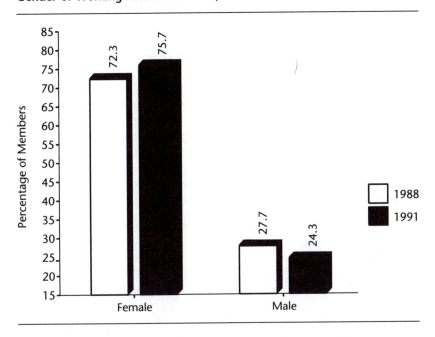

Gender, by Date of Highest Social Work Degree

As was just noted, the composition of the NASW membership is becoming more female, although women have been the majority of members since the association's inception (Becker, 1961). The feminization of the membership is highlighted when gender is examined in relation to the date of receipt of the highest social work degree. For example, in the 1991 data set, 37.8 percent (4,069) of those who received their highest degree between 1961 and 1970 were men. Furthermore, men constituted 30 percent or more of the membership from 1931 to 1976, with the notable exception of the period 1941 to 1950. The decrease in the proportion of male members receiving their degrees in those years should be viewed within the context of World War II and the proportion of all U.S. men then serving in the military.

In sharp contrast are findings for 1986 to 1990, when 19.9 percent (4,077) of those who obtained their highest degrees were men. For those who received their degrees after 1990, the proportion of men

37

TABLE 3.1

Gender, by Ethnicity of Working NASW Members

	1988				1991			
	Female		Male		Female		Male	
	n	%[a]	*n*	%[a]	*n*	%[a]	*n*	%[a]
American Indian	201	70.3	85	29.7	321	76.6	98	23.4
Asian	689	70.9	283	29.1	902	72.8	337	27.2
African American	2,648	77.8	756	22.2	3,781	80.6	908	19.4
Chicano	327	60.8	211	39.2	510	63.7	291	36.3
Puerto Rican	325	74.5	111	25.5	476	77.4	139	22.6
Other Hispanic	332	74.6	113	25.4	600	77.7	172	22.3
White	40,710	88.8	14,905	88.8	56,861	76.3	17,703	23.7
Other	612	73.2	314	26.8	767	68.4	355	31.6
Total number and percentage of respondents[b]	45,844	73.2	16,778	26.8	64,218	76.2	20,003	23.8

[a] Percentage responding to both gender and ethnicity.
[b] Total responding to both gender and ethnicity, 1988 = 62,622, 1991 = 84,221.

dropped to 14.7 percent (719). The downward trend in the ratio of male to female members has been consistent since 1961 (see Figure 3.2).

The feminization of the NASW membership is further discernible when gender is examined in relation to age. The proportion of male NASW members aged 35 and over (27.1 percent) is significantly higher than the proportion of men under age 35 (14.9 percent). This finding is consistent with the findings that related gender to the date of the highest social work degree. In 1991, the percentage of female members aged 45 and under was 63.8; the percentage of male members in this age group was 58.9. The percentage of female members aged 36 and over was 74.0, whereas that of males over age 35 was 86.3. Thus the proportion of female members was much higher in the younger age groups and the proportion of male members higher in the older age groups (see Table 3.2).

In 1991, women made up 70 to 75 percent of most age categories. However, there were exceptions found at both ends of the age continuum. In the over-70 category, 80.9 percent of the members were female, perhaps because of the longer life span of American women.

FIGURE 3.2

Gender of Working NASW Members, by Date of Receipt of the Highest
Degree, 1991

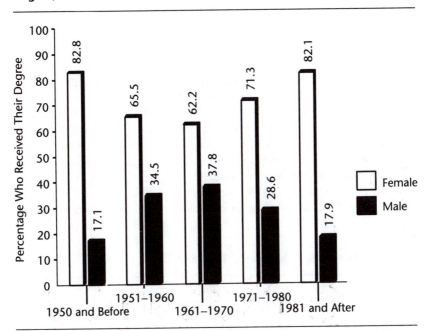

TABLE 3.2

Gender by Age of NASW Members, 1991

Age	Female		Male		Total Responding	
	n	%	n	%	n	%
Under 26 years	2,773	85.1	182	14.9	2,955	3.4
26–35 years	14,586	83.7	2,848	16.3	17,434	19.8
36–45 years	25,073	72.6	9,463	27.4	34,536	39.2
46–50 years	10,964	74.6	3,727	25.4	14,691	16.7
51–60 years	10,302	71.4	4,124	28.6	14,426	16.4
Over 60 years	2,905	73.8	1,030	26.2	3,935	4.5
Total	66,603	75.7	21,374	24.3	87,977	100.0

In the 21–30 category, 89.1 percent of the members were female. This finding may further document the continuing feminization of the NASW membership.

AGE

Shifts in the age of NASW members may be signaling a trend counter to that of the general population. Whereas the general population is aging, more NASW members are younger. The median age of employed NASW members in both 1988 and 1991 was 41 to 45. However, in 1991, 41.6 percent of the 92,155 members (38,303) who responded were 40 or younger, compared to 34.8 percent (26,929) of the 77,075 members who responded in 1988 (see Figure 3.3).

As expected, members whose highest degree is the BSW tend to be younger than the other NASW members. In 1988, 27.0 percent (998) of the 3,696 BSW members who responded were aged 21 to 30, com-

FIGURE 3.3

Age of Working NASW Members, 1988 and 1991

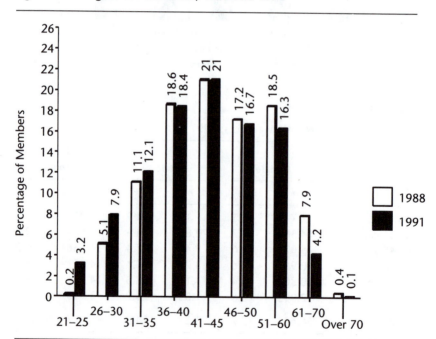

pared to 38.3 percent (1,881) of the 4,911 BSW members who responded in 1991 (see Table 3.3).

For both 1988 and 1991, the majority of those holding doctoral degrees were aged 41 to 60. Still, the trend toward younger NASW members is also observed at this degree level. In 1988, 9.5 percent (283) of the 2,970 members with doctorates who responded were aged 31 to 40, compared to 13.9 percent (522) of the 3,750 members with doctorates who responded in 1991. The trend is also evident among the younger group with doctoral degrees. In 1988, 0.5 percent (14) of the members with doctorates who responded were aged 21 to 30, compared to 1.0 percent (35) in 1991.

Age, by Date of Highest Social Work Degree

As expected, there is a high correlation between the age of members and the date at which they obtained their highest social work degree. However, as Table 3.4 shows, in 1991, a significant number of members were in the category of "nontraditional" students, who tended to be older than the norm of those in graduate school when they completed their social work education and thus did not go directly from undergraduate to graduate education. For example, 28.9 percent of those aged 51 to 60 received their highest social work degree in the 1970s, when they were 30 to 40 years old. Similarly, 36.3 percent of those aged 41 to 50 and 29.0 percent of those aged 51 to 60 received their highest social work degree after 1980, again when they were over 30 years old. Furthermore, age in relation to the date of receipt

TABLE 3.3

Age, by Highest Social Work Degree, 1988 and 1991 (percentage)

Age	BSW 1988	1991	MSW 1988	1991	DSW–PhD 1988	1991
21–30 years	27.0	38.3	3.7	10.0	0.5	1.0
31–40 years	29.5	28.5	30.3	31.3	9.5	13.9
41–50 years	22.1	21.2	39.3	38.3	45.0	47.6
51–60 years	14.7	9.6	18.6	16.2	28.0	28.3
Over 60 years	6.8	2.3	8.2	4.3	17.0	9.3
Total respondents	3,696	4,911	66,342	82,633	2,970	3,750
Percentage	5.1	5.4	90.9	90.5	4.1	4.1

TABLE 3.4

Age Group, by Date of Receipt of Highest Social Work Degree, 1991 (percentage)

	Date of Highest Social Work Degree				
Age	Before 1950	1951–60	1961–70	1971–80	1981–90
21–30 years	0.0	0.1	0.4	1.5	77.2
31–40 years	0.0	0.1	0.4	29.9	64.4
41–50 years	0.1	0.2	13.7	46.1	36.3
51–60 years	0.2	8.4	31.6	28.9	29.0
Over 60 years	3.8	25.5	22.9	30.6	16.8
Total respondents	214	2,217	9,735	27,386	39,767
Percentage	0.2	2.6	11.6	32.5	53.0

of the highest social work degree may reflect career changes after several years of work experience or the fulfillment of family obligations before the pursuit of professional education.

It is interesting to note that the closest association between age and the date of receipt of the highest social work degree was found for those aged 21 to 30, 77.2 percent (7,617) of whom earned their degrees between 1981 and 1990. In contrast, of those aged 41 to 50, 46.1 percent (11,605) earned their degrees between 1970 and 1980. And of those aged 51 to 60, 31.6 percent (4,365) earned their degrees between 1961 and 1970.

ETHNICITY

The ethnic composition of the NASW membership was overwhelmingly white—88.5 percent—in 1988 and 1991. Approximately 78 percent (67,123) of the 1988 data set of 86,091 employed members responded to the question about ethnicity (see Figure 3.4), with a higher proportion of respondents in 1991, at 84 percent (84,685) of the 1991 data set of 100,899.

The proportion of people of color remained basically unchanged from 1988 to 1991. African Americans represented 5.6 percent of the respondents in both 1988 (3,784) and 1991 (4,713). Hispanics, including Chicanos, Puerto Ricans, and other Hispanics, constituted 2.3 percent (1,560) of the respondents in 1988 and 2.5 percent (2,196) in

FIGURE 3.4

Ethnicity of Working NASW Members, 1988 and 1991

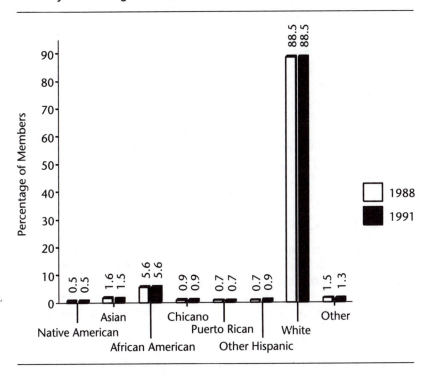

1991. Among the Hispanic groups in both years, Chicanos were the largest proportion—0.9 percent (588 in 1988 and 804 in 1991). Asians represented 1.6 percent (1,046) of the respondents in 1988 and 1.5 percent (1,252) in 1991.

Ethnicity, by Date of Highest Social Work Degree

Several notable trends emerge when ethnicity is examined in relation to the date of receipt of the highest social work degree. Although still a small proportion of the total membership, the proportion of other Hispanic members has increased consistently since 1951. Of those who earned their highest degree before 1950, 0.5 percent (one member) identified himself or herself as other Hispanic, compared to 1.3 percent (509) of those who earned their highest degree after 1980.

There has also been an upward trend in the proportion of Chicano and Puerto Rican members, although to a lesser degree than the proportion of members in the other Hispanic category (see Table 3.5).

There has been a decrease in the proportion of African American NASW members. Of those who earned their highest degree between 1971 and 1980, 6.5 percent (1,678) were African American, compared to 5.0 percent (523) who did so after 1980.

Overall, NASW does seem to be attracting ethnic minority graduates in the same proportion as it is white graduates. CSWE (Spaulding, 1991) reported that from 1986 to 1991, 13.9 to 18.5 percent of the social work degrees were issued to members of ethnic minority groups. This ratio is slightly higher than the 11.5 percent of the NASW members who reported being members of ethnic minority groups in both 1988 and 1991.

Ethnicity, by Experience

Native Americans, Puerto Ricans, and other Hispanics have been recruited into the profession and to NASW membership in recent years. The level of experience of these three groups of members was concentrated in the under-10-years category in 1991. The highest proportion of Chicanos had six to 20 years of experience, whereas the highest

TABLE 3.5

Ethnic Group, by Date of Receipt of Highest Social Work Degree, 1991 (percentage)

Ethnic Group	Before 1950	1951–60	1961–70	1971–80	1981–90
	\multicolumn{5}{c}{Date of Highest Social Work Degree}				
Native American	0.0	0.5	0.3	0.5	0.6
Asian	1.0	2.7	2.0	1.5	1.3
African American	6.7	8.3	5.5	6.5	5.0
Chicano	0.0	0.3	0.5	1.0	1.1
Puerto Rican	0.0	0.4	0.5	0.7	0.8
Other Hispanic	0.5	0.3	0.4	0.7	1.3
White	0.3	86.0	89.4	87.4	88.9
Other	0.8	1.4	1.3	1.6	1.1
Total respondents	222	2,206	9,366	25,743	40,622
Percentage	0.2	2.8	12.0	33.0	52.0

proportions of African American, white, and Asian members had between 11 and 15 years and over 26 years of experience.

EDUCATION

The vast majority of the employed NASW members who responded to this question—90.5 percent (72,946 out of 80,633) in 1988 and 90.4 percent (90,092 out of 99,619) in 1991—had an MSW as their highest degree (see Figure 3.5). The proportion of members at the doctoral level has remained constant in both years at 4.3 percent (3,435 in 1988 and 4,314 in 1991).

In light of the proliferation of BSW programs in the past two decades, the absolute and proportional representation of BSWs in the NASW membership is surprisingly low. In fact, there was a slight decrease from 1988 to 1991 in the proportion of employed members whose highest degree was the BSW: from 5.3 percent (4,252) of the respondents in 1988 to 5.2 percent (5,213) in 1991. From 1986 to

FIGURE 3.5

Highest Social Work Degree of Working NASW Members, 1988 and 1991

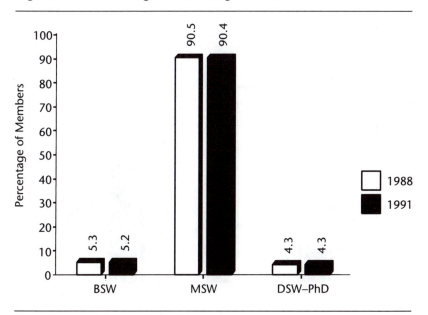

1990, CSWE (Spaulding, 1991) reported that 34,319 BSW degrees were issued by the 366 accredited BSW programs in the United States. Obviously, NASW is not attracting members of this group.

Gender, by Highest Degree

Proportionately more men than women obtain doctoral degrees in social work (see Figure 3.6). Of the members who had a PhD or DSW, 48 percent (1,413) were male and 52 percent (1,530) were female in 1988 and 45 percent (1,764) were male and 55 percent (2,159) were female in 1991—a small but positive change in the proportion of woman who obtained doctorates. The fact remains, however, that the number of men with PhDs or DSWs was disproportionate to their overall representation in the membership.

The proportion of male members whose highest degree was the BSW also deviated from the proportion of men in the overall membership, but in the opposite direction. Of those whose highest degree was the BSW, 17.5 percent (598) were male and 82.5 (2,821) were female

FIGURE 3.6

Degree, by Gender of Working NASW Members, 1991

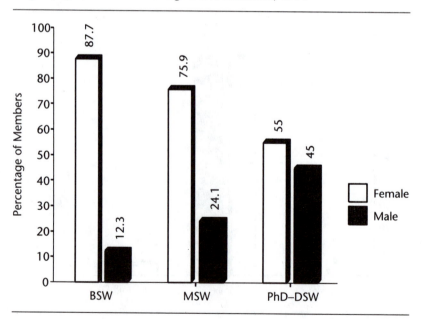

in 1988 and 12.3 (615) were male and 87.7 percent (4,378) were female in 1991. Thus, the proportion of men at the BSW level decreased from 1988 to 1991.

Date of Highest Social Work Degree

Because many social work students enter graduate school as part of a career change or to initiate a first career after raising a family, the date of receipt of the highest social work degree is a more accurate demographic variable than is age by which to profile the NASW members. This variable provides information about when members entered the professional social work labor force (see Table 3.6).

In 1988, the median period in which the highest degree was obtained was 1971–75, whereas in 1991 it was 1981–90. Of the 1991 data set, 64.1 percent (58,922) received their highest social work degree between 1976 and 1990, compared to 47.4 percent (27,982) in the 1988 data set. These findings suggest that a significant proportion of the members join NASW soon after they receive their highest degree, but may not remain members for many years. The trend to discontinue membership appears to have strengthened between 1988 and 1991. In 1991, the largest proportion and number of members received their highest social work degrees in the 1986–90 period,

TABLE 3.6

Date of Receipt of the Highest Social Work Degree, 1988 and 1991

	1988		1991	
	n	%[a]	*n*	%[a,b]
Before 1951	1,027	1.7	388	0.5
1951–1960	4,149	7.0	2,956	3.2
1961–1970	13,084	22.1	11,910	12.9
1971–1975	12,824	21.7	12,890	14.0
1976–1980	14,063	23.8	17,202	18.7
1981–1985	6,839	11.6	16,433	17.9
1986–1990	7,080	12.0	25,287	27.5
After 1990	71	0.1	4,947	5.4
Total respondents	59,137		92,013	

[a] Percentage of respondents for year.
[b] Percentages do not total 100 because of rounding.

whereas in 1988 the largest proportion of members received their highest social work degree between 1976 and 1980.

These findings suggest that the recruitment of members is most successful immediately or soon after a prospective member completes his or her degree. NASW's recruitment strategies may have been particularly successful after 1985. In 1991, those who received their highest social work degree after 1985 represented 32.9 percent (30,234) of the employed membership, whereas in 1988 they accounted for only 13.4 percent (8,151).

GEOGRAPHIC DISTRIBUTION OF MEMBERS

The highest proportion of the employed respondents—23.2 percent (23,346)—resided in the Mid-Atlantic states in 1991, compared to 24.2 percent (20,738) in 1988 (see Tables 3.7 and 3.8). The second-ranked region of NASW membership was the East North Central region, where 18.8 percent (18,902) of the 100,547 respondents resided in 1991, compared to 19.3 percent (16,535) of the 85,712 respondents in 1988. The third largest region was the South Atlantic, which, unlike

TABLE 3.7

Geographic Distribution of Working Members, 1988 and 1991

	1988		1991	
Region	*n*	%ª	*n*	%
New England	9,112	10.6	10,519	10.5
Mid-Atlantic	20,738	24.2	23,346	23.2
East North Central	16,535	19.3	18,902	18.8
West North Central	5,502	6.4	6,465	6.4
South Atlantic	11,773	13.7	14,652	14.6
East South Central	2,461	2.9	3,043	3.0
West South Central	5,414	6.3	6,578	6.5
Mountain	3,632	4.2	4,576	4.6
Pacific	10,465	12.2	12,395	12.3
Territories	80	0.1	71	0.1
Total respondents	85,712		100,547	

ª Percentages do not total 100 because of rounding.

TABLE 3.8

States by Region

New England	Minnesota	**West South Central**
Connecticut	Missouri	Arkansas
Maine	Nebraska	Louisiana
Massachusetts	North Dakota	Oklahoma
New Hampshire	South Dakota	Texas
Rhode Island	**South Atlantic**	**Mountain**
Vermont	Delaware	Arizona
Mid-Atlantic	District of Columbia	Colorado
New Jersey	Florida	Idaho
New York	Georgia	Montana
Pennsylvania	Maryland	Nevada
East North Central	North Carolina	New Mexico
Illinois	South Carolina	Utah
Indiana	Virginia	Wyoming
Michigan	West Virginia	**Pacific**
Ohio	**East South Central**	Alaska
Wisconsin	Alabama	California
West North Central	Kentucky	Hawaii
Iowa	Mississippi	Oregon
Kansas	Tennessee	Washington

the Mid-Atlantic and East North Central regions, experienced a small increase from 1988 to 1991—13.7 percent (11,773) in 1988 to 14.6 percent (14,652) in 1991.

Geographic Region, by Degree

An examination of geographic region in relation to the type of degree held by NASW members yields some interesting revelations. For example, since the Mid-Atlantic states are much more densely populated than are the Mountain states, conventional wisdom would suggest that (1) the proportion of NASW members in any given geographic region would be roughly proportionate to the proportion of the U.S. population in that region and (2) the proportion of BSWs, MSWs, and PhDs–DSWs to the total NASW membership would be roughly equivalent in each region.

This second assumption does not hold up. The largest proportion of BSW members did not reside in the regions with the highest composite NASW membership in 1991. For example, in 1991, 6.4 percent (6,380) of the 99,272 NASW members who responded resided in the West North Central region, but a disproportionate 14.4 percent (749) of the 5,201 BSW members who responded lived there. A disproportionately high number of BSW members, compared to the total NASW members in a region, were also found in the East North Central, East South Central, West South Central, and Mountain regions. On the other hand, there were disproportionately fewer BSW members in the New England, Mid-Atlantic, and Mountain regions. BSWs were an approximately equal proportion of the total NASW membership only in the South Atlantic and West South Central regions (see Table 3.9).

The proportion of MSWs and PhD–DSWs in each region were roughly equivalent to the proportion of NASW members residing in each region in 1991. Thus, the disparities at the BSW level may point to untested differences in the job market for BSW graduates in the regions. For example, it is possible that in regions other than New England and North Central, where the not-for-profit sector is most firmly entrenched, social services are provided primarily by the public

TABLE 3.9

Degrees of NASW Working Members in Each Region, 1991 (percentage)

Region	BSW	MSW[a]	DSW–PhD
New England	6.7	10.8	9.0
Mid-Atlantic	15.8	23.5	25.5
East North Central	23.1	18.7	15.6
West North Central	14.4	6.0	5.5
South Atlantic	15.0	14.5	16.0
East South Central	4.9	2.9	3.0
West South Central	8.0	6.5	6.9
Mountain	6.3	4.4	5.1
Pacific	5.7	12.7	13.2
Territories	0.0	0.1	0.2
Total respondents	5,201	89,795	4,276
Percentage	5.2	90.5	4.3

[a] Percentages do not total 100 because of rounding.

sector, which tends to employ proportionately more BSW members than do other sectors (see Chapter 4). There may be more employment opportunities for BSW social workers in these regions.

EXPERIENCE

There was a downward trend in the level of experience of NASW members from 1988 to 1991. The median level of experience was 11 to 15 years in 1991 versus 16 to 20 years in 1988 (see Table 3.10).

Eighty-four percent of the total 1991 data set and 57.5 percent of the total 1988 data set of employed NASW members responded to the question about experience. In 1991, 44.9 percent (38,004) of the 84,792 respondents indicated that they had 10 or fewer years of experience—a sharp contrast to 1988, when only 17.3 percent of the 49,545 respondents (8,563) indicated this level of experience. There was also a sharp contrast between the higher levels of experience in these two years. In 1991, only 36.2 percent (30,727) of the respondents had 16 or more years of experience, compared with 59 percent (29,251) in 1988.

Experience, by Highest Social Work Degree

As Table 3.11 indicates, the NASW membership was less experienced in 1991 than in 1988. For all degrees, the proportion of members

TABLE 3.10

Experience of Working NASW Members, 1988 and 1991

Years of Experience	1988		1991		% Change
	n	%	n	%	
Less than 2	122	0.2	9,388	11.1	+11.8
2–5	3,799	7.7	14,734	17.4	+9.7
6–10	4,642	9.4	13,882	16.4	+7.0
11–15	11,731	23.7	16,061	18.9	−4.8
16–20	11,699	23.6	13,439	15.8	−7.8
21–25	8,242	16.6	8,976	10.6	−6.0
More than 25	9,310	18.8	8,312	9.8	−9.0
Total respondents	49,545		84,792		

TABLE 3.11

Degree, by Years of Experience of Working NASW Members, 1988 and 1991 (percentage)

Years of Experience	BSW		MSW		DSW–PhD	
	1988	1991	1988[a]	1991	1988[a]	1991
Less than 2	5.4	63.6	0.3	11.6	0.0	0.6
2–5	56.9	18.1	8.1	18.0	0.8	3.3
6–10	13.7	8.8	9.8	16.8	2.4	6.5
11–15	10.6	4.0	24.3	19.1	13.4	16.5
16–20	5.1	2.3	23.6	15.4	24.5	25.4
21–25	5.6	2.1	16.3	10.1	21.6	21.0
More than 25	2.7	1.1	17.7	9.0	37.2	26.7
Total respondents	663	1,791	46,655	80,859	2,890	3,833
Percentage	5.0	3.3	93.7	94.6	1.3	2.1

[a] Percentages do not total 100 because of rounding.

increased in the lower levels of experience and decreased in the higher levels. For example, in 1988, 62.3 percent of the respondents whose highest social work degree was a BSW had five or fewer years of experience, compared to 81.7 percent in 1991. Although the general level of experience increased with each degree, the trend toward less experience continued across all degrees. For those with MSW degrees, 8.4 percent reported five or fewer years of experience in 1988 versus 29.6 percent in 1991.

The more experienced NASW respondents were those with doctoral degrees in both years. For example, 37.2 percent of the PhDs or DSWs had over 26 years of experience in 1988, compared to 17.7 percent of the MSWs. This finding is not surprising because doctoral-level members tend to be older than MSW- or BSW-level members and age is positively associated with experience. However, the trend was not as pronounced in 1991 as in 1988. In 1991, 26.7 percent of those with PhDs or DSWs had over 26 years of experience, compared to 9 percent with MSWs.

Experience, by Date of Highest Social Work Degree

When experience is analyzed in relation to the date of receipt of the highest social work degree, the findings are also in the predicted direction. The respondents who earned their degrees in earlier years had more experience in 1991. Of those who earned their highest degrees between 1986 and 1990, 64.4 percent (14,296) had two to five years of experience. Of those who earned their highest degree between 1976 and 1980, 88.9 percent (14,352) had 11 to 15 years of experience. And, of those who earned their degree between 1961 and 1970, 64.8 percent (7,290) had 21 to 25 years of experience.

Experience, by Gender

When experience is examined in relation to gender, the findings reveal expected patterns. As was discussed earlier, since a higher proportion of male members were aged 41 and older in 1991, it is not surprising that men were generally more experienced. Indeed, the proportion of women with 10 or fewer years of experience was consistently higher than the proportion of men in each years-of-experience category (under two years, two to five years, and so on) whereas the proportion of men was consistently higher than that of women in every years-of-experience category from 11–15 years and over.

CHAPTER HIGHLIGHTS: 1988 TO 1991

- The proportion of women members increased.
- The largest proportion of male members were aged 35 to 45, compared to 31 to 40 for female members.
- There were proportionately fewer African American male members and more Chicano male members than those of other ethnic groups in the NASW membership.
- The NASW membership was overwhelmingly white.
- The proportion of Hispanic members, particularly other Hispanic members, increased.
- The proportion of people of color who were NASW members was only slightly lower than the proportion of people of color who received social work degrees.
- The proportion of African American members decreased.
- The median age of NASW members decreased.
- Those whose highest social work degree was the BSW tended to be the youngest members.

- The trend toward a younger population of NASW members was also evident at the doctoral level.
- Over 90 percent of the NASW membership had an MSW as their highest social work degree.
- Approximately 4 percent of the members were at the doctoral level.
- In absolute and proportional numbers, BSWs were under-represented in the membership compared to the number of BSW degrees awarded.
- Proportionally more men than women in the membership had doctoral degrees in social work.
- Proportionally more women than men in the membership had BSW degrees.
- A significant proportion of members joined NASW soon after they received their highest degrees.
- A significant number of members cease to be members after several years of membership.
- The highest proportion of members lived, in rank order, in the Mid-Atlantic, East North Central, and South Atlantic regions.
- The proportion of MSWs and PhDs–DSWs in each region was approximately equivalent to the proportion of members residing in each region.
- The proportion of BSW members in each region did not mirror their proportion in the NASW membership.
- The level of experience of NASW members decreased.
- Doctoral-level members had the most years of experience, but the trend was less pronounced in 1991 than in 1988.

REFERENCES

Becker, R. (1961, Spring). *Study of salaries of NASW members*. New York: National Association of Social Workers.

Spaulding, E. (1991). *Statistics on social work education in the United States: 1990*. Alexandria, VA: Council on Social Work Education.

CHAPTER 4

WHERE WE WORK

AUSPICE AND SETTING

PRIMARY AUSPICE

NASW delineates seven categories for the auspice, or operating authority, of social work practice: public local, public state, public federal, public military, private not-for-profit sectarian, private not-for-profit nonsectarian, and private for-profit. NASW members are asked to indicate, from these categories, the auspice under which they work.

Social work practice is predominantly carried out under the aegis of public, not-for-profit, and for-profit organizations. When the nonsectarian and sectarian categories were combined, private not-for-profit organizations ranked first among auspices in 1991, representing 32,246 (38.9 percent) of the 82,880 respondents. Public auspices (government) at the combined local, state, federal, and military levels ranked second, representing 37.2 percent (30,881) of the respondents (see Table 4.1).

From 1988 to 1991, there was a slight but significant decrease in the proportion of NASW members employed by the various levels of government. In 1988, 40.4 percent (26,944) of the respondents indicated that they were employed by federal, state, or local government or the military. A slight decrease was also found for the proportion of respondents who were employed by sectarian and nonsectarian not-for-profit organizations in that period: from 39.8 percent (26,623) in 1988 to 38.9 percent (32,246) in 1991.

In contrast, the proportion of respondents who worked under private for-profit auspices increased between 1988 and 1991—from 19.8 percent (13,223) to 23.8 percent (19,753).

Rankings by individual categories for 1988 and 1991 were consistent: private not-for-profit, private for-profit, and public local ranked

TABLE 4.1

Primary Auspice of Working NASW Members

Primary Auspice	1988		1991	
	n	%	*n*	%[a]
Public local	12,309	18.4	15,368	18.5
Public state	11,937	17.9	12,461	15.0
Public federal	2,185	3.3	2,399	2.9
Public military	513	0.8	653	0.8
Private not-for-profit sectarian	7,697	11.5	10,078	12.2
Private not-for-profit nonsectarian	18,926	28.3	22,168	26.7
Private for profit	13,223	19.8	19,753	23.8
Total respondents	66,790		82,880	

[a] Percentages do not total 100 because of rounding.

first, second, and third, respectively. The growing proportion of
NASW members employed by private for-profit organizations suggests
that, contrary to historical patterns, the for-profit sector has evolved
into a major employer of social workers. This rise in for-profit employment may be attributed, in part, to changes in regulations that
have opened the door to third-party payments and vendorship for social work practitioners and, in part, to the growth in purchase-of-
service contracting between government and not-for-profit and for-
profit service providers. It is possible, however, that many respondents
did not accurately distinguish for-profit and not-for-profit auspices because they were not familiar with these terms.

Primary Auspice, by Highest Social Work Degree

The primary auspice differs to some extent according to the members'
highest level of social work education. For example, in 1991 the largest proportion of BSW respondents—25.3 percent (952)—cited public
local (government) as their primary auspice. The primary auspice of
the second highest proportion of BSW respondents—24.2 percent
(910)—was the private not-for-profit sector. The primary auspice of
the majority of MSW respondents, on the other hand, was the private
not-for-profit sector—27.1 percent (20,223)—followed by the private
for-profit sector—24.3 percent (18,110) (see Table 4.2).

TABLE 4.2

Primary Auspice of Working NASW Members, by Degree, 1991
(percentage)

Primary Auspice	BSW	MSW	PhD–DSW
Public local	25.3	18.6	10.0
Public state	17.3	14.2	29.2
Public federal	2.4	2.9	2.5
Public military	0.4	0.8	1.8
Private not-for-profit sectarian	14.3	12.1	10.2
Private not-for-profit nonsectarian	24.2	27.1	22.1
Private for profit	16.0	24.3	24.2
Total respondents	3,756	74,598	3,624
Percentage	4.6	91.0	4.4

In 1991, the largest proportion of doctoral-level members were employed in the public state (government) sector—a surprising finding. However, it is possible that many faculty at publicly supported universities list their auspice as state government. The second highest proportion of doctoral-level members—24.2 percent (878)—worked under private for-profit auspices. This finding may reflect a relatively large number of PhD–DSW members in private solo or group practice or, as with state government, teaching at private universities.

It is interesting that the highest proportion of the respondents who were working under military auspices were PhDs–DSWs. Although the total number employed by the military was relatively small, there was a discernible bias toward those holding a doctorate, perhaps because of financial support provided by the military to pursue doctoral studies.

Primary Auspice, by Experience

Two patterns can be observed when examining the experience of NASW members by the auspice of their primary employment. First, the distribution of working members by auspice reinforces the fact that the NASW membership is becoming less experienced. For every auspice, there was a significant increase in the percentage of members with less experience from 1988 to 1991. Second, there was an identifiable pattern of less-experienced members working with traditional agency-based clients. In 1991, the largest proportion of respondents in

57

most auspices had 11 to 15 years of experience. Deviating from this pattern were the public local and private not-for-profit (both sectarian and nonsectarian) auspices in which the largest proportion of respondents (32.9 and 30.8 percent, respectively) had five or fewer years of experience (see Figure 4.1).

Primary Auspice, by Gender

A significantly higher proportion of men (42.2 percent, 8,328) than women (36.1 percent, 20,647) cited government (at the state, federal, or military level) as their primary auspice in 1991. This finding is consistent with the proportionately higher salaries offered by government and the higher salaries earned by male NASW members (see chapter

FIGURE 4.1

Experience of Working NASW Members, by Auspice, 1988 and 1991

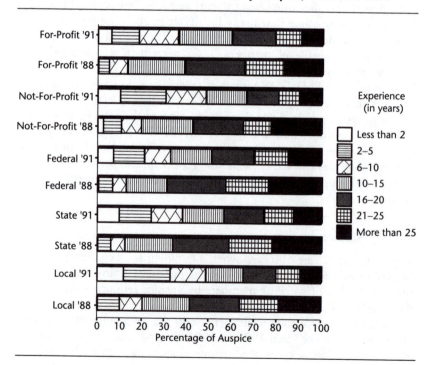

6). The proportion of women was higher in the private not-for-profit and private for-profit primary auspices (see Table 4.3).

Distinctions on the basis of gender were less notable for the secondary auspice than for the primary auspice. The most striking difference was in the private for-profit sector, where the proportion of men was higher. This is a reversal of the pattern for the primary auspice.

Primary Auspice, by Ethnicity

An examination of primary auspice in relation to the ethnicity of NASW members revealed some significant patterns. In 1991, a significantly higher proportion of people of color than of white people among the NASW membership were employed by the local, state, or federal governments. Furthermore, there were some distinctions based on the level of government. For example, a higher proportion of Asian, African American, Chicano, Puerto Rican, and other Hispanic members than other ethnic groups cited local government as their primary auspice. Except for other Hispanic, these same ethnic groups, notably African American and Asian members, had a higher ratio of employment in state government. In the private for-profit sector, there

TABLE 4.3

Primary Auspice of Working NASW Members, by Gender, 1991

Primary Auspice	Female		Male	
	n	%[a]	*n*	%
Public local	10,828	18.9	3,610	18.3
Public state	8,132	14.2	3,549	18.0
Public federal	1,369	2.4	872	4.4
Military	318	0.6	297	1.5
Public total	20,647	36.1	8,328	42.2
Private not-for-profit sectarian	7,046	12.3	2,360	12.0
Private not-for-profit nonsectarian	15,784	27.5	4,847	24.6
Not-for-profit total	22,830	39.8	7,207	36.6
Private for-profit	13,887	24.2	4,177	21.2
Total respondents	57,364		19,712	

[a] Percentages do not total 100 because of rounding.

were higher proportions of white and "other ethnic" members than of other ethnic groups (see Figure 4.2).

The patterns in relation to the secondary auspice by ethnicity are not identical to those for the primary auspice. In local government and in the military, there was a higher proportion of African American respondents in 1991, whereas in state government the proportion of Native American, Puerto Rican, and other Hispanic respondents was higher, and in the federal government the proportion of Native American, Asian, and African American respondents was higher than those of other ethnic groups (see Figure 4.3).

As was noted, the for-profit sector ranked first among the respondents who cited a secondary auspice. In this category, however, the white respondents had the highest proportional representation of all the ethnic groups.

SECONDARY AUSPICE

The trend away from the traditional government and not-for-profit bases of social work practice and toward the private for-profit sector was pronounced in relation to the secondary auspice. Of the 22,550 respondents who identified a secondary auspice in 1991 (22 percent of the data set of employed social workers), 11,184 (49.6 percent) reported the auspice to be private for-profit and 49 percent (8,468) of the 17,268 respondents did so in 1988. This category may include both organizational settings and individual or group private practice (see Table 4.4).

The second-ranked secondary auspice in both 1988 and 1991 was the not-for-profit sector. When the sectarian and nonsectarian auspices were combined, 28.6 percent (4,943) of the 1988 respondents and 28.4 percent (6,406) of the 1991 respondents reported that they worked under not-for-profit auspices. The third-ranked auspice for both years was government (federal, state, local, and military) at 22 percent (4,960) in 1991 and 22.4 percent (3,857) in 1988. On the basis of individual categories, the 1988 and 1991 rankings were also consistent: private for-profit, private not-for-profit, and public local, respectively.

The number of social workers who identified a public (local, state, or federal) secondary auspice in both 1988 and 1991 is surprising because the government is not typically a secondary employer. It is possible that a significant proportion of the members who listed their secondary auspice as public provide consultation or contract services.

FIGURE 4.2

Ethnic Composition of Primary Auspice of Working NASW Members, 1991

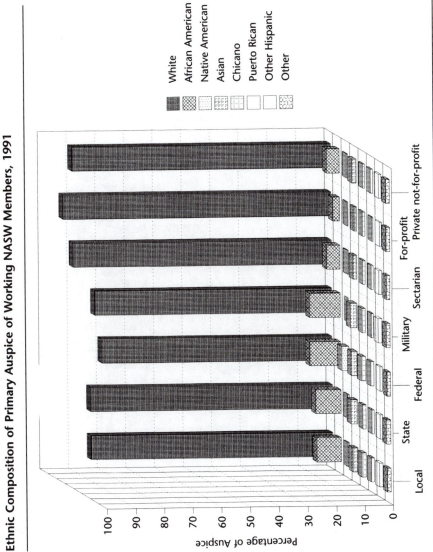

FIGURE 4.3

Minority Composition of Primary Auspice of Working NASW Members, 1991

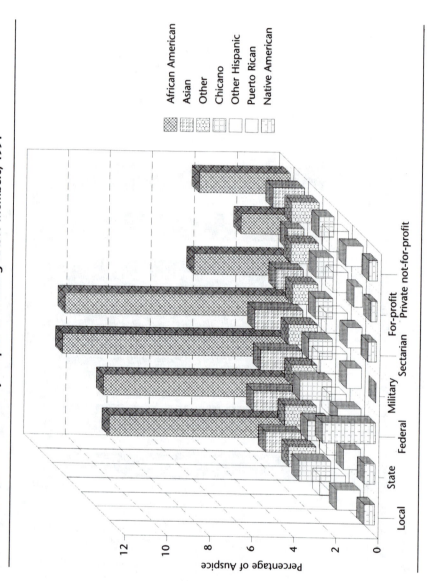

TABLE 4.4

Secondary Auspice of Working NASW Members

Secondary Auspice	1988		1991	
	n	%	*n*	%
Public local	1,693	9.8	2,243	9.9
Public state	1,687	9.8	2,139	9.5
Public federal	345	2.0	379	1.7
Public military	132	0.8	199	0.9
Private not-for-profit sectarian	1,403	8.1	1,940	8.6
Private not-for-profit nonsectarian	3,540	20.5	4,466	19.8
Private for-profit	8,468	49.0	11,184	49.6
Total respondents	17,268		22,550	

Secondary Auspice, by Degree

When the secondary auspice is examined in relation to the highest degree held, more information is available about the members who identified their secondary auspice as government. The largest proportion of respondents who identified any level of government as their secondary auspice were at the BSW level. For example, 18 percent (109) of the BSW respondents listed public local government as their secondary auspice, versus 9.9 percent (2,010) of the MSW respondents. The secondary auspice of public state government was identified by 21.2 percent (128) of the BSW respondents, compared to 9.1 percent (1,842) of the MSW respondents. Similar findings for the secondary auspice of federal government and military reveal a significantly higher proportion of BSW respondents than MSW or PhD–DSW respondents (see Table 4.5).

The absolute and proportionate number of respondents whose secondary auspice was private for-profit is noteworthy. In 1991, the private-for-profit sector ranked first as the secondary auspice across all educational levels: BSWs, 23.1 percent (140); MSWs, 50.5 percent (10,270); and PhDs–DSWs, 48.2 percent (672).

PRIMARY SETTING OF PRACTICE

Of the 13 settings of social work practice identified by NASW, agencies ranked first in both 1988 and 1991, representing 24.4 percent

TABLE 4.5

Secondary Auspice of Working NASW Members, by Degree, 1991

Secondary Auspice	BSW	MSW	PhD–DSW
Public local	18.0	9.9	6.7
Public state	21.2	9.1	11.3
Public federal	4.0	1.6	2.2
Public military	2.3	0.9	0.8
Private not-for-profit sectarian	11.1	8.5	9.0
Private not-for-profit nonsectarian	20.3	19.7	21.9
Private for-profit	23.1	50.5	48.2
Total respondents	605	20,336	1,395
Percentage[a]	2.7	91.0	6.2

[a] Percentages do not total 100 because of rounding.

(16,353) of the 66,887 respondents in 1988 and 22.8 percent (19,589) of the 86,006 respondents in 1991. Hospitals ranked second in both study years, at 20.7 percent (13,831) of the respondents in 1988 and 20.9 percent (17,951) in 1991. Clinics ranked third in both years, at 17.1 percent, for 11,448 of the respondents in 1988 and 14,731 in 1991. However, 14.8 percent (9,881) of the respondents in 1988 and 16.8 percent (14,430) in 1991 cited private solo and private group, combined; thus, this category evidenced the largest proportional growth of any primary setting between 1988 and 1991 (see Table 4.6).

Primary Setting, by Degree

There are significant differences in the primary setting of practice based on the highest degree held. Considerably fewer PhD–DSW respondents than BSW or MSW respondents worked in organizational settings (agencies, hospitals, institutions, nursing homes, and group homes) in 1991 (see Table 4.7). The vast majority of them were in universities (36.7 percent) or private solo (17.2 percent) or private group (4.3 percent) practice. This finding confirms earlier hypotheses that members at the doctoral level report their auspice based on the public versus private nature of their employing institutions of higher education.

An examination of the data on primary practice settings reinforces the view that clients with the most complex and intractable socioeco-

TABLE 4.6

Primary Setting of Working NASW Members

Primary Setting	1988		1991	
	n	%	*n*	%
Agency	16,353	24.4	19,589	22.8
Private solo	6,968	10.4	10,458	12.2
Private group	2,913	4.4	3,972	4.6
Membership organization	536	0.8	639	0.7
Hospital	13,831	20.7	17,951	20.9
Institution	2,070	3.1	2,514	2.9
Clinic	11,448	17.1	14,731	17.1
Group home	1,459	2.2	1,967	2.3
Nursing home	1,424	2.1	2,018	2.3
Court	960	1.4	1,209	1.4
University	3,375	5.0	3,719	4.3
School	3,962	5.9	5,332	6.2
Non–social work setting	1,588	2.4	1,907	2.2
Total respondents	66,887		86,006	

Note: Percentages do not total 100 because of rounding.

nomic and psychosocial problems are served by the least educated members. Compared to MSWs and PhD–DSWs, more BSWs work in agencies, institutions, group homes, nursing homes, and courts— settings that are more likely than others to serve young, old, poor, and mentally and physically disabled people. Proportionally more BSW members are found in non–social work settings, and few BSWs work in primary solo or group practice.

Primary Setting, by Date of Highest Social Work Degree

When primary practice settings are examined in relation to the date of receipt of the highest social work degree, some trends, but few startling findings, emerge. There is a slight tendency for the more recent graduates to work in agencies and a more pronounced tendency for them to work in hospitals, institutions, group homes, and nursing homes.

In contrast, those who have been out of school the longest and hence have the greatest amount of experience tend to be in private

TABLE 4.7

Primary Setting of Working NASW Members by Degree, 1991

Primary Setting	BSW	MSW	PhD–DSW
Agency	34.0	22.7	11.4
Private solo	2.2	12.5	17.2
Private group	0.7	4.9	4.3
Membership organization	0.6	0.8	0.8
Hospital	16.9	21.5	10.7
Institution	3.9	2.9	1.7
Clinic	9.9	17.9	9.7
Group home	7.5	2.1	0.4
Nursing home	12.5	1.9	0.6
Court	2.5	1.4	0.8
University	2.4	2.8	36.7
School	3.1	6.5	3.4
Non–social work setting	3.8	2.1	2.3
Total respondents	3,997	77,260	3,775
Percentage	4.7	90.9	4.4

solo practice, universities, and schools, whereas those who earned their highest degree between 1961 and 1985 tend to work in private group practice. These findings suggest that NASW members typically begin their professional practice in organizational settings and then move into private group practice and finally into private solo practice.

Trends in regard to secondary practice setting are consistent with primary setting. Members who received their highest social work degree in 1985 or earlier tended to cite private solo practice as their secondary practice setting. Members also tended to enter private solo practice sooner after graduation as a secondary rather than primary practice setting.

Primary Setting, by Experience

When the experience of NASW members is viewed in relation to their primary practice setting, the patterns are similar to those found for the date of receipt of the highest social work degree. Of those who responded to the questions about experience and primary setting in 1991 (73,388), the largest group—22.2 percent (16,311)—reported agencies as their primary setting. Of those who worked in agencies, 34.1 percent had fewer than five years of experience, whereas 20.6 percent had more than 20 years of experience. Other organizational settings demonstrated similar high proportions of members with less experience (see Figure 4.4).

Major shifts in the primary setting of NASW members can be seen at two and five years of experience. In 1991, the proportion of the respondents in private group practice increased significantly from 3.2 percent with fewer than two years' experience to 11.2 percent with

FIGURE 4.4

Experience of Working NASW Members, by Setting, 1991

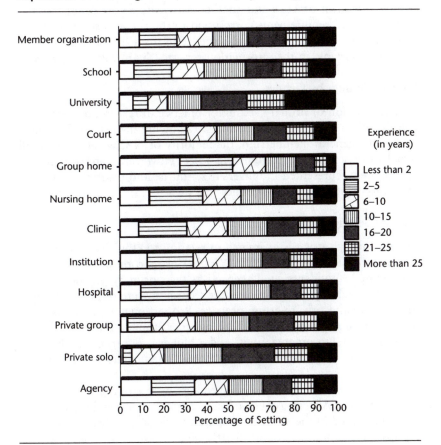

two to five years' experience. Similarly, those in private solo practice increased from 5.2 percent with fewer than five years' experience to 14.7 percent with six to 10 years' experience. All other social work settings experienced a drop in the percentage of respondents reporting six to 10 years of experience compared to those reporting fewer than six years' experience. This is a reversal of the patterns reported by the members in 1988.

The effects of licensing on the practice of social work, at least for NASW members, may account for these shifts in primary setting by experience. That is, NASW's considerable efforts to influence states to adopt professional regulation statutes for social workers have opened the door to private group and solo practice for social workers. In most instances, the laws require two years of supervised experience before semi-independent practice and another two years before unsupervised practice. These requirements correspond to the shifts in settings observed at two and five years of experience in the 1991 data set, but are not observable in the information reported by members in 1988.

Primary Setting, by Gender

An examination of primary setting of practice in relation to gender reveals only a few distinctive patterns. Following the gender distribution of the general membership, the majority of NASW members in all social work settings were women in 1991. However, men were disproportionately represented in universities, courts, and institutions and underrepresented in nursing homes (see Figure 4.5).

Primary Setting, by Ethnicity

When primary setting is examined in relation to ethnicity, patterns are similar for both 1988 and 1991. A higher proportion of nonwhite than white respondents cited agencies as their primary practice setting, whereas a higher proportion of white than nonwhite respondents cited private solo and private group practice. Proportionately, twice as many Chicano respondents as those of other ethnic groups of color listed membership organizations, and a higher proportion of Chicano, Puerto Rican, and other Hispanic members cited clinics (see Figure 4.6).

African American and Chicano members were overrepresented in the courts, and African American and Puerto Rican members were overrepresented in the schools compared to those of other ethnic groups. In addition, a proportionately higher number of Asian, Afri-

FIGURE 4.5

Gender of Working NASW Members, by Setting, 1991

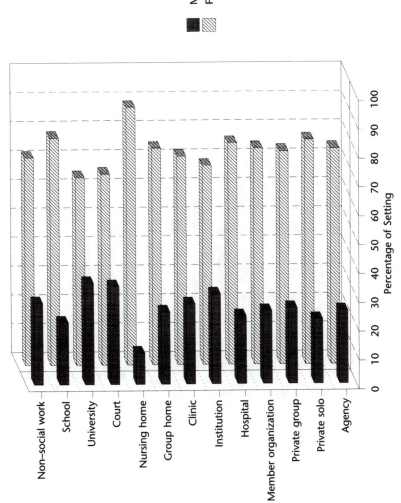

FIGURE 4.6

Ethnic Composition of Primary Setting of Working NASW Members, 1991

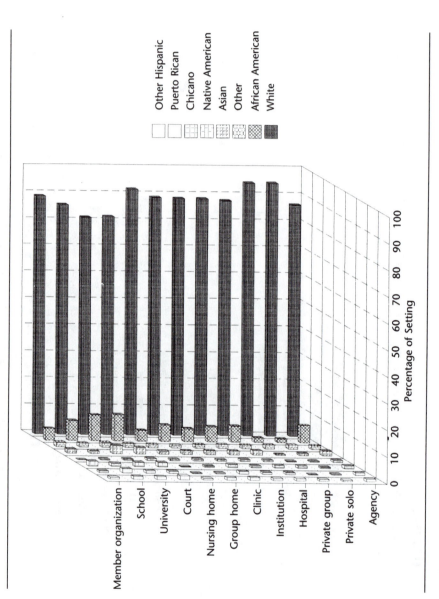

can American, and Chicano members than of other ethnic groups worked in universities (see Figure 4.7).

SECONDARY SETTING OF PRACTICE

Approximately 26 percent (22,384) of the data set of 86,091 employed NASW members in 1988 and 28 percent (28,252) of 100,899 employed members in 1991 responded to the question about a secondary setting of practice. The trend toward the private practice of social work is highlighted by the proportion of respondents who indicated private practice, individual or group, as their secondary setting: 45.8 percent of the respondents in both years. Thus, 10,087 respondents in 1988 and 12,786 in 1991 engaged in part-time private practice to augment their income and experience from their primary practice in an organizational setting (see Table 4.8).

Private solo practice ranked first among secondary settings of practice, followed, in both 1988 and 1991, by clinics, private group practice, and agencies. In 1991, 2,177, or 7.8 percent of the respondents, and in 1988, 7.9 percent of the respondents (1,738) identified universities as their secondary practice setting. These data suggest that schools of social work frequently hire practitioners as adjunct faculty for fieldwork supervision or classroom teaching.

Secondary Setting, by Degree

The findings regarding secondary practice setting and primary practice setting by degree are consistent. In 1991, the BSW respondents more than the MSW or PhD–DSW respondents reported agencies, membership organizations, hospitals, institutions, group homes, nursing homes, courts, schools, and non–social work settings as their secondary settings. The majority of MSW respondents with a secondary setting worked in private solo or group practice and clinics: 34.1 percent (8,583) in private solo practice, 12.7 percent (3,191) in private group practice, and 13.1 percent (3,295) in clinics (see Table 4.9).

The majority of PhD–DSW respondents with a secondary practice setting also worked in private or solo group practice in 1991: 34.7 percent in private solo practice and 10.5 percent in private group practice. Universities were also a major secondary setting for doctoral-level members, at 21.1 percent.

FIGURE 4.7

Minority Composition of Primary Setting of Working NASW Members, 1991

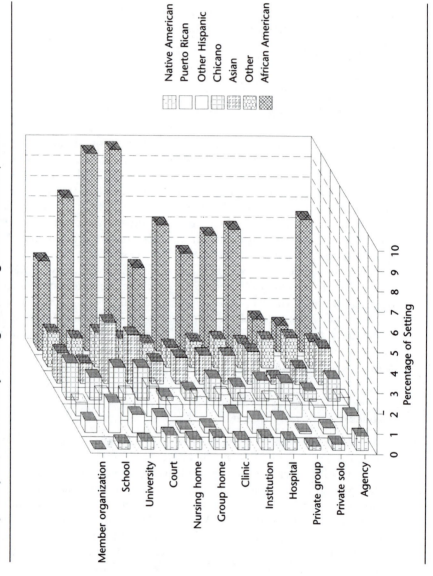

TABLE 4.8

Secondary Setting of Working NASW Members

Secondary Setting	1988		1991	
	n	%	*n*	%
Agency	2,103	9.6	2,815	10.1
Private solo	7,396	33.6	9,325	33.4
Private group	2,691	12.2	3,461	12.4
Membership organization	200	0.9	267	1.0
Hospital	1,451	6.6	2,064	7.4
Institution	464	2.1	573	2.1
Clinic	2,758	12.5	3,545	12.7
Group home	578	2.6	741	2.7
Nursing home	794	3.6	911	3.3
Court	390	1.8	460	1.6
University	1,738	7.9	2,177	7.8
School	475	2.2	716	2.6
Non–social work setting	949	4.3	881	3.3
Total respondents	21,987		27,936	

Note: Percentages do not total 100 because of rounding.

Secondary Setting, by Gender

The findings for secondary setting by gender differ from those for primary setting. A higher proportion of women worked in the secondary settings of agencies, clinics, nursing homes, and schools in 1991, whereas only nursing homes and schools as primary settings had a higher proportion of women. The proportion of men in the secondary settings of private solo and private group practice was higher—a reversal of the proportions found in these primary-setting areas—and in universities.

Secondary Setting, by Ethnicity

The pattern for secondary versus primary settings in relation to the ethnicity of members is not identical, although there is some overlap. A higher proportion of African American and Chicano respondents in 1991 cited agencies as their secondary setting, and a higher proportion of other Hispanic, white, and "other ethnicity" members cited private

TABLE 4.9

Secondary Setting of Working NASW Members by Degree, 1991

Secondary Setting	BSW	MSW	PhD–DSW
Agency	18.0	9.9	9.4
Private solo	8.2	34.1	34.7
Private group	5.2	12.7	10.5
Membership organization	2.5	0.9	1.2
Hospital	9.3	7.5	5.1
Institution	4.2	2.0	1.8
Clinic	12.7	13.1	6.9
Group home	13.8	2.4	1.3
Nursing home	8.3	3.3	1.4
Court	4.6	1.6	0.8
University	4.0	7.1	21.1
School	4.4	2.6	1.6
Non–social work setting	4.9	3.0	4.2
Total respondents	756	25,190	1,688
Percentage	2.7	91.2	6.1

solo practice than did members of other ethnic groups. In contrast, a higher proportion of Chicano, Puerto Rican, and other Hispanic respondents than other respondents listed private group practice.

A higher proportion of other Hispanic respondents listed membership organizations as their secondary setting, and a higher proportion of Puerto Rican respondents cited institutions. There was a higher ratio of Native American, Asian, and other Hispanic respondents than respondents of other ethnic groups in hospitals and a higher proportion of Native American and African American respondents in clinics. A higher proportion of Native American, African American, Chicano, and Puerto Rican respondents than respondents of other ethnic groups cited the courts, and a higher proportion of Native American, Asian, and African American respondents listed universities.

CHAPTER HIGHLIGHTS

- The not-for-profit sector (sectarian and nonsectarian combined) was the auspice of practice for the largest proportion of NASW members.

- The second-ranked auspice was government at the combined local, state, federal, and military levels.

- By individual categories, the members identified their work auspice, in rank order, to be private not-for-profit, private for-profit, and public local.

- The proportion of members working under a governmental auspice and for not-for-profit organizations decreased.

- The proportion of members working under private for-profit auspices increased.

- The primary auspices differed on the basis of the highest social work degree held. The majority of BSWs cited local government, followed by the private not-for-profit sector; the majority of MSWs cited private not-for-profit, followed by the private for-profit sector; the majority of PhDs–DSWs cited state government (but this surprising finding may include publicly supported universities).

- The highest proportion of members working for the military were at the doctoral level.

- The less experienced members worked in traditional social work agencies.

- A higher proportion of male members than female members reported their primary auspice as government.

- Proportionately more male members than female members indicated private for-profit as their secondary auspice.

- A higher proportion of members of color were employed by the local, state, or federal government.

- Proportionately more white members than those of other ethnic groups reported the private for-profit sector as their primary and secondary auspices.

- African American members had the highest proportional representation of any ethnic group in the military.

- Almost half the members who reported a secondary auspice identified it as the private for-profit sector.

- The second-ranked secondary auspice was the private not-for-profit (sectarian and nonsectarian) sector, and the third-ranked was the government.

- The largest proportion of members who identified government at any level as their secondary auspice were at the BSW level.
- Agencies were ranked first as the primary setting of social work practice, followed by hospitals and clinics.
- Private solo and private group practice evidenced the largest proportional growth between 1988 and 1991 of any primary setting.
- The vast majority of PhD–DSW members were in private solo or group practice or worked in a university.
- Proportionately more BSWs worked in agencies, institutions, group homes, nursing homes, and courts than did MSWs and PhDs–DSWs.
- More recent graduates and those with less experience tended to work in agencies and to have a primary practice setting of hospitals, institutions, group homes, and nursing homes.
- Those who earned their highest degree at earlier dates and had more years of experience were disproportionately represented among members whose primary setting was private solo practice.
- The members entered private solo practice as a secondary setting much sooner after graduation than as a primary setting.
- Male members were disproportionately represented in the primary practice settings of universities, courts, and institutions.
- A higher proportion of members of color cited agencies as their primary setting than did white members.
- A higher proportion of white members were in the primary settings of primary solo and private group practice.
- Approximately 46 percent of those who indicated they had a secondary setting were in private individual or group practice.
- The higher proportion of male members than of female members in private solo and group practice as a secondary setting reverses the proportions found for primary setting.

CHAPTER 5

WHAT WE DO

AREAS OF PRACTICE AND FUNCTIONS PERFORMED

FULL- VERSUS PART-TIME EMPLOYMENT

In 1991, 52 percent of the data set of employed NASW members responded to the question about their full- versus part-time employment
status; only 14.4 percent responded to this question in 1988. (It
should be noted that, on the membership application form, the question about full- versus part-time employment status is listed as a sub-
category of the question about current annual salary from primary
employment only; it is within the context of this question that the respondents were asked to indicate whether their annual salary is for
full- or part-time employment.)

Of the 52,717 NASW members who responded to this question in
1991, 78.8 percent (41,526) were employed full time and 21.2 percent
(11,191) were employed part time. For the 12,408 respondents in
1988, 81.4 percent (10,100) were employed full time and 18.6 percent
(2,308) were employed part time. These data suggest that the proportion of NASW members who are employed full time versus those who
are employed part time decreased slightly from 1988 to 1991. Given
the low response rate in 1988, however, such interpretations may be
unfounded (see Figure 5.1).

PRIMARY PRACTICE AREA

For both 1988 and 1991, the largest proportion of respondents were
in the primary practice area of mental health: 32.7 percent (28,545)
of the 87,265 respondents in 1991, compared to 31.3 percent (21,431)
of the 68,465 respondents in 1988. The second-ranked practice area
for both years was children—16.3 percent in both 1988 and 1991.

FIGURE 5.1

Employment Status of NASW Members

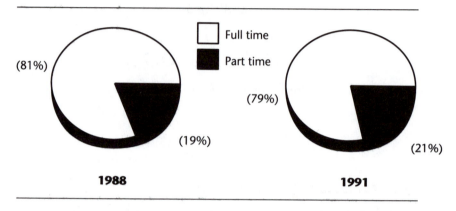

Medical clinics ranked third, and family services ranked fourth for both years, with little proportional variation (see Table 5.1).

Primary Practice, by Highest Degree Held

There are some noteworthy distinctions in the members' primary practice area on the basis of their highest degrees. In 1991, proportionately more BSW respondents designated public assistance, aged, and mental retardation–developmental disabilities as their primary practice areas, and proportionately fewer cited mental health. Proportionately more PhD–DSW respondents listed community organization–planning, occupational, "combined," and "other" as their primary practice areas, and proportionately fewer noted medical clinics.

The proportional differences in primary practice on the basis of highest degree may reflect a differential utilization pattern of personnel in human services agencies. Such a differential structure may not, however, be consistent with the standards set forth in NASW's *Standards for the Classification of Social Work Practice* (NASW, 1981). More information is needed about the distinctions among the functions performed in these primary settings through such means as job analysis.

As Table 5.2 shows, few NASW members worked in corrections, public assistance, mental retardation–developmental disabilities, and occupational social work in both years, and as was noted earlier,

TABLE 5.1

Primary Practice Areas of Working NASW Members

Primary Practice Area	1988		1991	
	n	%	*n*	%
Children	11,165	16.3	14,256	16.3
Community organization–planning	913	1.3	976	1.1
Family services	8,422	12.3	9,860	11.3
Corrections	899	1.3	1,025	1.2
Group services	351	0.5	399	0.5
Medical clinics	9,005	13.2	10,926	12.5
Mental health	21,431	31.3	28,545	32.7
Public assistance	613	0.9	695	0.8
School social work	2,918	4.3	4,083	4.7
Aged	3,227	4.7	3,970	4.5
Substance abuse	2,731	4.0	4,031	4.6
Mental–developmental disabilities	2,038	3.0	2,356	2.7
Other disabilities	364	0.5	460	0.5
Occupational social work	527	0.8	711	0.8
Combined	3,339	4.9	4,836	5.5
Other	522	0.8	136	0.2
Total respondents	68,465		87,265	

those who did so tended to be BSWs. In chapter 7, the impact of the declassification of social service positions is discussed as one explanation for the diminished number of professionally trained social workers in the public social services.

Primary Practice, by Date of Highest Social Work Degree

A few trends are discernible when primary practice area is analyzed in relation to the date of receipt of the highest social work degree. In the practice areas of children, aged, substance abuse, and mental retardation–developmental disabilities, recent graduates (those who received their highest social work degree after 1985) were proportionately overrepresented, whereas in mental health they were proportionately underrepresented.

The primary practice areas of community organization–planning and public assistance were largely composed of members who received

TABLE 5.2

Distribution of the Degrees, of Working NASW Members, by Primary
Practice Area, 1991 (percentage)

Primary Practice Area	BSW	MSW	DSW–PhD
Children	17.9	16.4	12.1
Community organization–planning	1.7	1.0	3.2
Family services	9.9	11.5	9.0
Corrections	1.9	1.1	1.2
Group services	0.5	0.4	0.9
Medical clinics	16.1	12.6	7.8
Mental health	13.2	33.6	35.9
Public assistance	2.2	0.7	0.8
School social work	2.2	4.8	3.7
Aged	12.7	4.2	4.2
Substance abuse	3.8	4.0	3.3
Mental–developmental disabilities	7.1	2.8	2.1
Other disabilities	0.8	0.5	0.3
Occupational social work	0.6	0.7	1.5
Combined	6.8	4.5	11.8
Other	2.4	0.7	2.9
Total respondents	4,041	78,641	3,612
Percentage	4.7	91.1	4.2

Note: Percentages do not total 100 because of rounding.

their highest social work degree in the 1960s and early 1970s—a finding that is consistent with the tendency of social workers to move
from direct practice to macro practice as their careers progress. The
practice area of school social work also included a large proportion of
members who received their degrees in the 1960s and 1970s, although
it also included more recent graduates.

Primary Practice, by Experience

When the experience of NASW members by primary practice area is
examined, patterns emerge that are similar to those found for date of
highest social work degree. The members whose primary practice
areas were children, aged, developmental disabilities, substance abuse,
and public assistance reported less experience, and those in mental

health, occupational social work, and medical clinics reported more experience than did members in other primary practice areas.

In addition, there is a discernible pattern of shifts in practice area similar to those identified in regard to practice setting (see chapter 4). There appears to be a shift away from the practice areas of children, aged, developmental disabilities, substance abuse, and public assistance between two and five years of experience. After five years, there is a noticeable increase in the proportion of NASW members in mental health practice (see Table 5.3).

Some alternative explanations can be derived for these findings. First, the predominately agency- and institution-based practice areas of

TABLE 5.3

Experience of Working NASW Members, by Primary Practice Area, 1991 (percentage; $N = 74,471$)

Primary Practice Area	Years of Experience			
	0–1	2–5	6–10	11 or more
Children	13.6	21.1	16.6	48.9
Community organization–planning	12.8	13.8	9.8	63.6
Family services	9.4	18.7	16.5	55.4
Corrections	12.5	16.4	12.8	58.4
Group services	6.1	18.7	14.7	60.4
Medical clinics	9.0	18.9	17.7	54.3
Mental health	6.0	14.7	17.3	62.0
Public assistance	15.7	8.8	8.5	67.0
School social work	7.1	16.7	15.3	60.9
Aged	14.0	20.0	16.2	49.9
Substance abuse	14.4	27.1	20.0	38.5
Mental retardation–developmental disabilities	14.9	18.6	14.7	51.8
Other disabilities	9.5	19.8	19.0	51.7
Occupational social work	8.6	21.9	19.0	50.6
Combined	10.1	14.3	15.0	60.6
Other	0.0	0.0	1.7	98.3
Total respondents	7,029	13,189	12,448	41,805
Percentage[a]	9.4	17.7	16.7	56.1

[a]Percentages do not total 100 because of rounding.

children, aged, developmental disabilities, substance abuse, and public assistance may be more receptive to hiring new and recent graduates than many other practice areas because of the sheer number of practitioners needed. Second, the low levels of pay may invite entry-level practitioners, rather than more experienced practitioners who have more mobility and marketability by virtue of their experience. After gaining experience in these primary practice areas, NASW members are likely to move into other areas of practice, thus making room for new graduates to assume these positions and thus continuing the cycle. The impact on the quality of services delivered by the least experienced workers to clients with intractable social problems is worthy of investigation.

Primary Practice, by Gender

NASW members' selection of practice areas seems to reflect a gender-based role distinction apparent in the population as a whole. Whether for reasons of opportunity or preference, women in this society are frequently the primary caretakers of the family and children, aged and sick. Information provided by NASW members in 1991 reflects these trends. Proportionately more female respondents than male respondents worked in the primary practice areas of family service, medical clinics, school social work, and aged. Male members were proportionately overrepresented in community organization–planning, corrections, substance abuse, and mental health practice (see Table 5.4).

Findings are similar in regard to secondary practice area. The practice areas of children, family service, group services, medical clinics, school social work, and aged show proportionately more women. Proportionately more male NASW members have secondary practice areas of community organization–planning, corrections, mental health, and substance abuse.

Primary Practice, by Ethnicity

There are some distinctive patterns when primary practice area is examined in relation to ethnicity. Compared to other ethnic groups, and excluding whites, a higher proportion of Asian, Chicano, Puerto Rican, and other Hispanic members identified their primary practice area as children. A higher proportion of Asian, African American, and Puerto Rican members worked in community organization–planning, and a higher proportion of African Americans worked in corrections and public assistance in 1988 and 1991. A higher proportion of white

TABLE 5.4

Gender, by Primary and Secondary Practice Areas of NASW Members, 1991 (percentage)

Practice Area	Primary Area		Secondary Area	
	Female	Male	Female	Male
Children	75.2	24.8	71.9	28.1
Community organization–planning	61.0	39.0	63.9	36.1
Family services	77.7	22.3	72.6	27.4
Corrections	59.9	40.1	58.5	41.5
Group services	65.8	34.2	76.8	23.2
Medical clinics	83.0	16.2	75.3	24.7
Mental health	71.4	28.6	68.0	32.0
Public assistance	65.2	34.8	70.3	29.7
School social work	78.3	21.7	77.4	22.6
Aged	84.8	15.2	79.1	20.9
Substance abuse	66.1	33.9	63.9	36.1
Mental retardation–developmental disabilities	73.5	26.5	71.7	28.3
Other disabilities	77.5	22.5	77.9	22.1
Occupational social work	67.8	32.2	62.5	37.5
Combined	74.0	26.0	72.3	27.7
Other	53.1	46.9	50.7	49.3
Total respondents	60,700	20,424	24,384	10,131
Percentage	74.8	25.2	70.6	29.4

members worked in mental health, and a higher proportion of Asian and African American members than other ethnic groups worked in medical clinics. Schools included a higher proportion of African American and Puerto Rican members, and the practice area of substance abuse included a higher proportion of Native American and Puerto Rican members (see Figures 5.2 and 5.3).

Primary Practice, by Age

The patterns that emerged in regard to primary practice area by age were similar to those reported in relation to primary practice by experience. The primary practice areas of children, aged, mental

FIGURE 5.2

Ethnic Composition of Primary Practice Areas of Working NASW Members, 1991

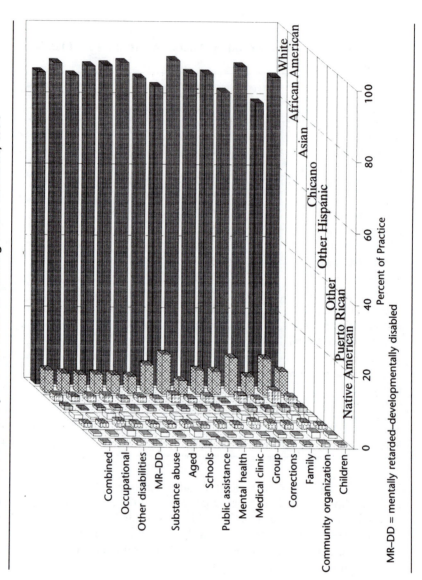

MR–DD = mentally retarded–developmentally disabled

FIGURE 5.3

Minority Composition of Primary Practice Areas of Working NASW Members, 1991

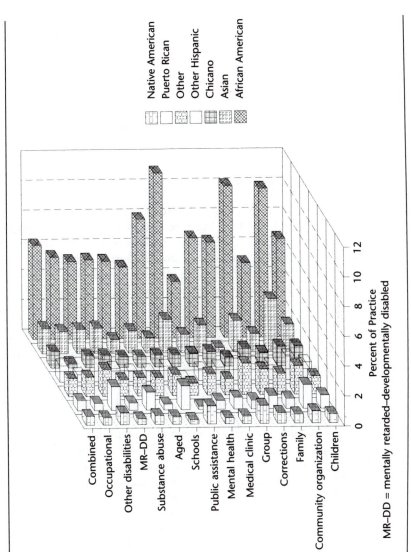

Native American
Puerto Rican
Other
Other Hispanic
Chicano
Asian
African American

Combined
Occupational
Other disabilities
MR–DD
Substance abuse
Aged
Schools
Public assistance
Mental health
Medical clinic
Group
Corrections
Family
Community organization
Children

0   2   4   6   8   10   12

Percent of Practice

MR–DD = mentally retarded–developmentally disabled

85

retardation–developmental disabilities, medical clinics, and substance abuse were likely to have a higher proportion of those aged 40 or under than were other practice areas. Members aged 41 or older were more likely to be found in community organization–planning, mental health, family services, public assistance, or combined areas. The finding in regard to public assistance was unexpected, but it may be that older members who work in the welfare system are in macro positions (see Figure 5.4).

SECONDARY PRACTICE AREA

Thirty-seven percent (37,322) of the total data set of employed NASW members indicated that they had a secondary practice area in 1991. For both 1988 and 1991, mental health, family service, children, and substance abuse were ranked first through fourth, respectively, as secondary areas of practice. Substance abuse was ranked considerably higher as a secondary than as a primary practice area (see Table 5.5).

Several alternative explanations exist for the relatively high proportion of NASW members who indicated a secondary practice area. First, professionals who are interested in more than one practice area may fulfill their occupational interests through part-time employment or consultation in a secondary setting.

Second, although members are asked on the NASW membership and renewal forms to indicate their practice area by their primary jobs and secondary jobs, if any, some members may respond to the question by indicating multiple areas of practice within their same (primary) employment setting. This possibility is enhanced by the number of social work practice settings (such as community mental health centers, family service agencies, and public social service agencies) that offer a diversity of services to a broad base of clients.

Third, the mobility in the profession may allow social workers to develop expertise in one practice area and then move to a new primary area of practice. In such instances, the members may classify their original primary practice area as "secondary." Fourth, because of their relatively low primary incomes, many NASW members may find it necessary to engage in a secondary income-producing activity.

Secondary Practice, by Degree

Consistent with the findings about the primary practice area by degree, there are also discernible trends among employed NASW

FIGURE 5.4

Age of Working NASW Members, by Primary Practice Areas, 1991

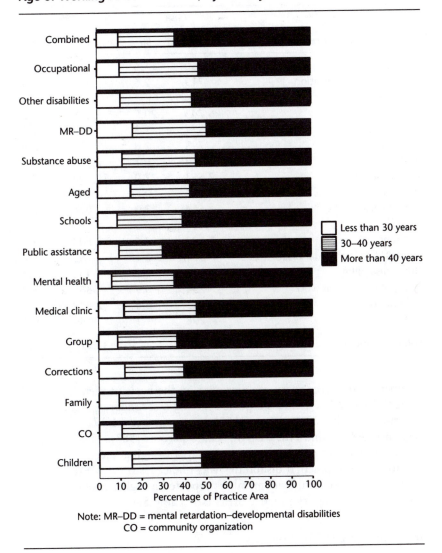

Note: MR–DD = mental retardation–developmental disabilities
CO = community organization

87

TABLE 5.5

Secondary Practice Area of Working NASW Members

Secondary Practice Area	1988		1991	
	n	%	*n*	%
Children	3,250	11.6	4,580	12.3
Community organization–planning	719	2.6	739	2.0
Family services	5,743	20.5	7,145	19.2
Corrections	377	1.3	500	1.3
Group services	793	2.8	1,029	2.8
Medical clinics	1,712	6.1	2,176	5.8
Mental health	7,553	27.0	10,328	27.7
Public assistance	166	0.6	234	0.6
School social work	554	2.0	814	2.2
Aged	1,684	6.0	1,953	5.2
Substance abuse	2,128	7.6	3,608	9.7
Mental–developmental disabilities	579	2.1	755	1.2
Other disabilities	346	1.2	452	1.2
Occupational social work	254	0.9	361	1.0
Combined	1,845	6.6	2,479	6.7
Other	298	1.1	69	0.2
Total respondents	28,001		37,222	

members with a secondary practice area on the basis of their highest degrees. In 1991, few BSWs reported having a secondary practice area in mental health—12.6 percent (157)—compared to MSWs—28.2 percent (9,489)—and PhDs–DSWs—29.8 percent (583). The proportion of BSWs with a secondary practice area of aging and mental retardation–developmental disabilities was higher than for MSWs and PhDs–DSWs. Doctoral-level members reported a higher proportion of "combined" secondary practice areas (see Table 5.6).

Secondary Practice, by Ethnicity

Some, but not all, of the patterns found for primary practice area by ethnicity were the same for secondary practice area. In 1988 and 1991, the secondary practice area of children included a higher proportion of African American, Puerto Rican, and "other" NASW

TABLE 5.6

Highest Social Work Degrees of Working NASW Members, by Secondary Practice Area, 1991 (percentage)

Secondary Practice Area	BSW	MSW	PhD–DSW
Children	15.4	12.2	11.6
Community organization–planning	3.5	1.8	3.3
Family services	19.1	19.4	14.5
Corrections	2.9	1.3	0.9
Group services	3.1	2.8	1.9
Medical clinics	7.7	5.8	5.8
Mental health	12.6	28.2	29.8
Public assistance	1.4	0.5	1.4
School social work	2.5	2.1	2.8
Aged	10.5	5.1	4.7
Substance abuse	7.4	9.9	8.4
Mental–developmental disabilities	4.2	2.0	1.7
Other disabilities	3.3	1.2	0.7
Occupational social work	1.0	0.9	1.5
Combined	5.2	6.5	10.3
Other	0.2	0.2	0.6
Total respondents	1,249	33,616	1,956
Percentage	3.4	91.3	5.3

members than of other ethnic groups. Community organization–planning included a higher proportion of Chicano, Puerto Rican, and "other" members, and family services included a higher proportion of Native American, Chicano, and other Hispanic members. Corrections included a higher proportion of African American, Chicano, and Puerto Rican members, and medical clinics included a higher proportion of Chicano, other Hispanic, and white members.

Consistent with the findings regarding primary practice areas, mental health as a secondary practice area included a higher proportion of white members, and school social work included a higher proportion of Native American, African American, and Chicano members. The highest proportion of those with a secondary practice area of substance abuse were Native Americans. Public assistance included a higher proportion of Asian, African American, Puerto Rican, and

Chicano members. Finally, services to the aged included a higher proportion of Asian and African American members than those of other ethnic groups.

PRIMARY FUNCTION

For both years, the overwhelming majority of respondents cited direct service as their primary function: 68.5 percent (60,904) of the 88,925 respondents in 1991 versus 65.1 percent (47,050) of the 72,239 respondents in 1988. The second-ranked category was management, representing 16.2 percent (14,365) of the respondents in 1991 and 17.7 percent (12,778) in 1988 (see Table 5.7).

These data suggest a significant skewing between direct (micro) and indirect (macro) functions in social work practice that is increasing with time. Policy, consultation, research, and planning functions combined represented only 2.7 percent (2,455) of the members in 1991 and 3 percent (2,159) in 1988. When management was factored in, the total for macro practice reached 18.9 percent (16,820) in 1991 and 20.7 percent (14,937) in 1988. From 1988 to 1991, there was a discernible downward trend in the proportion of members performing macro-level functions.

TABLE 5.7

Primary Function of Working NASW Members

Primary Function	1988		1991	
	n	%	*n*	%
Direct service	47,050	65.1	60,904	68.5
Supervision	4,592	6.4	5,456	6.1
Management	12,778	17.7	14,365	16.2
Policy	362	0.5	431	0.5
Consultation	1,170	1.6	1,286	1.4
Research	281	0.4	388	0.4
Planning	346	0.5	350	0.4
Education	3,281	4.5	3,719	4.2
Non–social work	2,379	3.3	2,026	2.3
Total respondents	72,239		88,925	

Primary Function, by Highest Social Work Degree

When primary function is examined according to the highest social work degree held, some interesting findings emerge. In 1991, direct service was the primary function for the majority of BSW (72.1 percent, or 2,997) and MSW respondents (69.7 percent, or 55,724). For PhDs–DSWs, it was the primary function for 39.1 percent (1,522) of the respondents. The second highest proportion of doctoral-level members—31.9 percent (1,241)—identified education as their primary function. This finding is not surprising. However, of those members whose primary function was education, 3.9 percent were BSWs and only 2.8 percent were MSWs. This finding suggests that education may have two definitions for NASW members: (1) education as school-based practice and (2) education as university teaching. Across the three educational levels, those with PhDs or DSWs were more likely to identify research as their primary function than were BSWs or MSWs (see Table 5.8).

In 1991, a relatively consistent proportion of the respondents at the three educational levels identified management as their primary function: 17.3 percent (672) of the PhDs–DSWs, 16.4 percent (13,133) of the MSWs, and 9.3 percent (387) of the BSWs. Although one would expect to find significantly more doctoral- than MSW- or BSW-level

TABLE 5.8

Highest Social Work Degrees of Working NASW Members, by Primary Function, 1991 (percentage)

Primary Function	BSW	MSW	PhD–DSW
Direct service	72.1	69.7	39.1
Supervision	5.1	6.3	3.0
Management	9.3	16.4	17.3
Policy	0.3	0.5	0.8
Consultation	0.8	1.5	2.1
Research	0.3	0.3	3.4
Planning	0.5	0.4	0.4
Education	3.9	2.8	31.9
Non-social work	7.6	2.0	2.1
Total respondents	4,154	79,895	3,893
Percentage	4.7	90.8	4.5

Note: Percentages do not total 100 because of rounding.

members with this function, almost the same proportion of managers are found in the degree category of BSWs and doctoral-level respondents. Put another way, about 5 percent of those with management as their primary function were BSWs and about 5 percent were PhDs–DSWs. The same finding holds true for those in supervision, where 2.9 percent of the supervisors were BSWs and 3.3 percent were PhDs–DSWs.

Primary Function, by Date of Highest Social Work Degree

When primary function is examined in relation to the date of receipt of the highest social work degree, several trends emerge. First, NASW members tend to assume the primary function of supervision after working in the field for several years; the majority of those in supervision completed their highest degree before 1980. The same pattern holds true for management, consultation, policy, and education (see Figure 5.5).

An unexpected finding was that the majority of respondents who reported the primary functions of research and planning earned their highest degree after 1980. This phenomenon may reflect the effects of changing priorities in the human services, where demands for accountability may have fostered a greater interest in research to demonstrate the effectiveness of practice. Similarly, the rate and intensity of legislative and regulatory changes at the federal, state, and local levels may have stimulated more interest in planning to implement new mandates.

Primary Function, by Experience

There are two significant observations about primary function in relation to years of experience. First, a decided shift in function occurs between two and five years of practice and between six and ten years of practice. The proportion of NASW members who reported supervision as their primary function increased sharply at two to five years of experience. Similarly, the proportion of members who reported management as a primary function increased at 11 to 15 years of experience. The fact that members move rapidly into supervision should alert social work education programs to the continued importance of post-degree opportunities for professional development and the need to enhance the curriculum on supervision. Furthermore, continuing education–professional development programs on management need to be developed and targeted to members from their sixth to tenth year of practice (see Figure 5.6).

FIGURE 5.5

Date of Highest Social Work Degree, by Primary Function of NASW Members, 1991

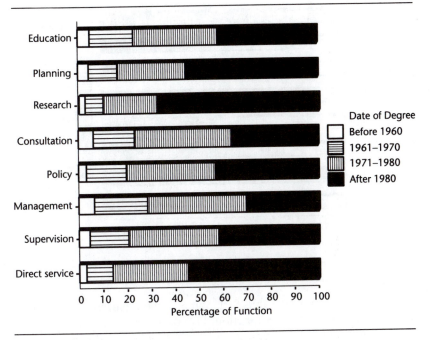

Another significant observation is that a large proportion of the respondents in research and planning reported fewer than two years of experience. As with the observations related to the date of the highest degree, the political climate may have influenced the functions of NASW members. An alternative explanation may be that graduates enter practice aware of and eager to practice a full range of social work functions, but after about five years of practice, career mobility, opportunities, and more specialized areas of interest move them into functions other than research and planning.

Primary Function, by Gender

In 1991, a significantly higher proportion of female than male respondents reported their function as direct service, whereas a higher proportion of male than female respondents cited supervision, manage-

93

FIGURE 5.6

Experience of Working NASW Members, by Function, 1991

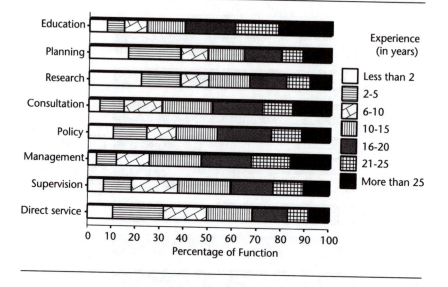

ment, or education (see Table 5.9). Some of these patterns are reversed in regard to the secondary function. Proportionately more male than female respondents reported the secondary function of direct service, and proportionately more female than male respondents cited the secondary function of education.

Primary Function, by Ethnicity

In 1991, a slightly higher proportion of Native American, Asian, African American, and Puerto Rican members than those of other non-white ethnic groups cited supervision as their primary function. At the direct-service level, there was a lower proportion of African Americans and a higher proportion of other Hispanics. The opposite trend was observed with regard to management, where a higher proportion of African Americans and a lower proportion of other Hispanics claimed that management was their primary function (see Figures 5.7 and 5.8).

Although only a small proportion of members reported their primary function as policy, a higher proportion of Native American and

TABLE 5.9

Gender of Working NASW Members, by Primary Functions, 1991

Primary Function	Female		Male	
	n	%	*n*	%
Direct service	44,770	72.4	11,882	57.1
Supervision	3,567	5.8	1,479	7.1
Management	7,991	12.9	5,330	25.6
Policy	271	0.4	127	0.6
Consultation	882	1.4	297	1.4
Research	259	0.4	104	0.5
Planning	257	0.4	71	0.3
Education	2,270	3.7	1,177	5.7
Non–social work	1,612	2.6	349	1.7
Number and percentage of respondents	61,879	74.8	20,816	25.2

Asian members cited it. In consultation there was a higher proportion of Native American members, and in research a higher proportion of Asian members than those of other ethnic groups. A higher proportion of African American and Asian members also cited their primary function as education.

SECONDARY FUNCTION

Approximately 48 percent (43,205) of the 1991 data set of employed social workers reported a secondary function—a significant proportional increase over the 39 percent (33,745) of the 1988 data set of employed members who reported a secondary function. Although the question pertaining to the secondary function refers to the function, if any, performed in a secondary job, the respondents may have reported a secondary function in their primary job that they considered to be of equal weight. Therefore, caution must be applied when interpreting these data because it is not known whether responses relate to a primary function in a secondary setting or a secondary function in a primary setting.

For both years, direct service was most frequently cited as the primary function in a secondary job: by 32.8 percent (14,151) of the

FIGURE 5.7

Ethnic Composition of Primary Functions of Working NASW Members, 1991

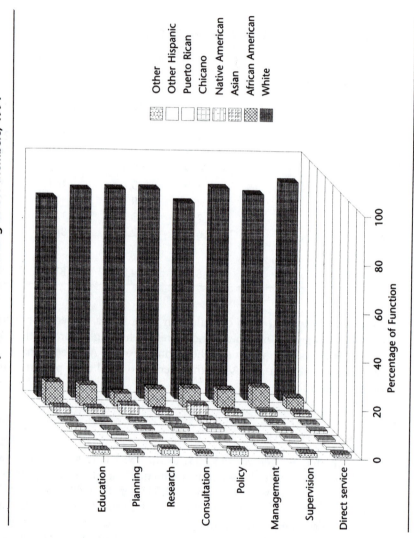

FIGURE 5.8

Minority Composition of Primary Functions of Working NASW Members, 1991

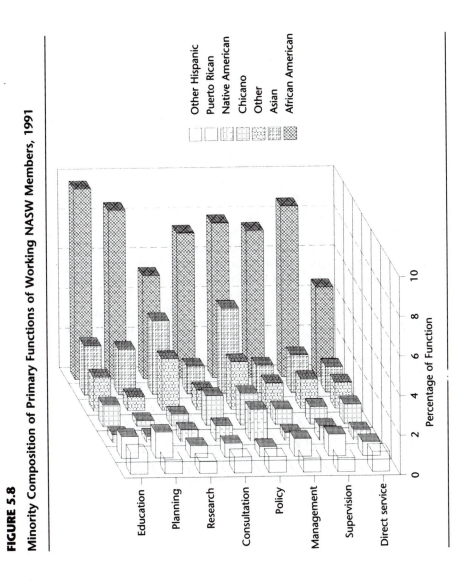

respondents in 1991 and 33.3 percent (11,235) in 1988. For both
years, supervision ranked second, at 19.5 percent (8,443) in 1991 and
18.4 percent (6,194) in 1988 (see Table 5.10).

A higher proportion of members carry out functions associated with
macro-level practice in their secondary than in their primary jobs. (It
should be noted that the issue of whether respondents reported a primary function of a second job or a secondary function of a primary
job is particularly relevant here.) In 1991, 30.6 percent (13,255) of the
respondents reported management, policy, consultation, research, or
planning as their secondary function, compared to 31 percent (10,464)
in 1988. Of these, 14.4 percent (6,217 in 1991, 4,862 in 1988) cited
consultation as that function in 1991 and 1988.

The finding that 15.2 percent (6,563) of the respondents in 1991
and 14.7 percent (4,974) of the respondents in 1988 reported education as their primary function in a second job suggests that a significantly higher proportion of members work as educators in secondary
rather than in primary jobs. Only 4.2 percent (3,719) of the respondents in 1991 and 4.5 percent (3,281) in 1988 identified education as
their primary function (see Table 5.7). These part-time educators may
be associated with social work education programs as adjunct faculty
or may engage in education as a secondary function of a primary job
(for example, a direct service practitioner who is secondarily responsi-
ble for staff development and in-service training). Correlations reveal a

TABLE 5.10

Secondary Function of Working NASW Members

Secondary Function	1988		1991	
	n	%	n	%
Direct service	11,235	33.3	14,151	32.8
Supervision	6,194	18.4	8,443	19.5
Management	3,403	10.1	4,336	10.0
Policy	790	2.3	957	2.2
Consultation	4,862	14.4	6,217	14.4
Research	641	1.9	838	1.9
Planning	768	2.3	907	2.1
Education	4,974	14.7	6,563	15.2
Non–social work	878	2.6	793	1.8
Total respondents	33,745		43,205	

high degree of consistency between the primary and secondary functions.

Secondary Function, by Degree

When secondary function is examined in relation to the highest degree held by NASW members, some surprising findings emerge. Of the 10 percent (4,291) of the respondents who cited management as a secondary function in 1991, 8.9 percent (229) were PhDs–DSWs, 10 percent (3,882) were MSWs, and an unexpected 13 percent (180) were BSWs. It is also surprising that the largest proportion of members who cited both policy and planning as their secondary function and a significantly higher proportion of those with a non–social work secondary function were BSWs. Again, it is possible that some respondents were indicating these functions as secondary functions in a primary job, whereas others were indicating them as primary functions in a secondary job (see Table 5.11).

More in line with conventional wisdom is the finding that the majority of those who cited research as a secondary function were at the doctoral level. Another expected finding is that the largest proportion of members in all three educational levels listed direct service as their secondary function.

TABLE 5.11

Highest Social Work Degrees of Working NASW Members, by Secondary Function, 1991 (percentage)

Secondary Function	BSW[a]	MSW	PhD–DSW
Direct service	27.5	33.2	29.8
Supervision	17.2	20.2	10.7
Management	13.0	10.0	8.9
Policy	4.3	2.1	2.9
Consultation	8.9	14.5	15.0
Research	1.7	1.3	12.3
Planning	4.6	2.0	1.3
Education	17.6	14.9	18.1
Non–social work	5.1	1.8	1.0
Total respondents	1,383	38,745	2,581
Percentage[a]	3.2	90.7	6.0

[a]Percentages do not total 100 because of rounding.

99

The tendency for NASW members who received their highest social work degree in earlier years to cite supervision, management, policy, and consultation as their secondary functions is consistent with the findings for primary function in relation to the date of receipt of the highest degree. But those with a secondary function of education tended to be more evenly distributed along the continuum of degree dates.

Secondary Function, by Ethnicity

The findings regarding secondary function by ethnicity sometimes overlap with, but are by no means identical to, those in relation to primary functions. As expected, the proportion of all ethnic groups with a secondary function of direct service was high. A lower proportion of Asian and other Hispanic members, however, cited this function. Also, a lower proportion of Native American and Chicano members reported supervision as a secondary function.

The proportion of Chicano members in management and the proportion of Chicano and other Hispanic members in consultation as secondary functions were higher than those of other ethnic groups. Although policy ranked relatively low as a secondary function for all ethnic groups, the proportion of Asian, African American, and other Hispanic members in this function was higher than for other ethnic groups.

The proportion of Asian members with a secondary function of research was significantly higher and the proportion of Puerto Rican members with a secondary function of planning was higher than for other groups, whereas the proportion of Native American and other Hispanic members was higher in education.

Despite the significant differences in primary and secondary functions by ethnicity, there is no clear explanatory variable. The lack of consistency between the primary and secondary functions by ethnicity suggests that the patterns are illusive.

CHAPTER HIGHLIGHTS

- The primary practice area of the highest proportion of NASW members was mental health, followed by children, medical clinics, and family services.
- A higher proportion of BSW members than of MSW or PhD–

DSW members reported public assistance, aged, and mental retardation–developmental disabilities as their primary practice areas.

- A higher proportion of doctoral-level members than BSW or MSW members were in the primary practice areas of community organization–planning, occupational social work, "combined" areas, or "other" areas.
- Among those who received their highest degree in earlier years, a higher proportion reported community organization–planning, public assistance, and mental health as their primary practice areas than did the more recent graduates.
- Those who received their highest degree relatively recently cited children, aged, and mental retardation–developmental disabilities, as well as substance abuse as their primary practice areas.
- Proportionately more female than male members reported the primary practice areas of family services, medical clinics, school social work, and aged.
- Among the distinctions in primary and secondary practice areas on the basis of ethnicity, a higher proportion of white members than those of other ethnic groups were in mental health practice.
- Older members were concentrated in the practice areas of mental health, community organization–planning, family services, public assistance, and "combined" areas.
- Thirty-seven percent of the employed NASW members had a secondary practice area.
- Among the secondary practice areas, mental health, family services, children, and substance abuse, respectively, were ranked the highest.
- Among the differences in secondary practice areas were that proportionately fewer BSWs were in the secondary practice area of mental health and proportionately more BSWs were in the secondary practice area of aging or mental retardation–developmental disabilities.
- The overwhelming majority of members reported their primary function as direct service, and direct service was the modal response for BSW, MSW, and doctoral-level members.
- A significantly higher proportion of female than male members cited their primary function as direct service.
- The second-ranked primary function was management.

- The proportion of members in direct versus indirect service increased from 1988 to 1991.
- The primary functions of less than 3 percent of the members were policy, consultation, research, or planning.
- Doctoral-level members were more likely than were BSW or MSW members to identify research as their primary and secondary function.
- The proportion of members at the three educational levels who identified management as their primary function was relatively consistent.
- The career path of NASW members appears to follow a predictable and sequenced pattern of direct service, supervision, management, consultation, education, and policy.
- The proportion of members who reported a secondary function increased significantly between 1988 and 1991.
- Direct service was the most frequently identified secondary function.
- A higher proportion of members cited macro-level practice as a secondary function than as a primary function.

CHAPTER 6

WHAT WE EARN

INCOME OF NASW MEMBERS

This chapter presents information about the salaries that NASW members earned in 1988 and 1991. Although NASW conducted a salary study using membership profiles for July 1, 1986, through June 30, 1987, comparisons to 1988 and 1991 are difficult. The data analysis conducted for the 1986–87 study was based on an earlier version of the members' demographic survey form. The following data limitations were noted:

> Although the database contains information related to respondents' primary employment only, the questions on the data-gathering instruments did not ask respondents to indicate if their primary employment was on a full-time or part-time basis. As a result, the database contains salary information for respondents employed on both a full-time and part-time basis. Although the number of respondents employed on a less than full-time basis is believed to be relatively small, some skewing of the data results from including part-time salaries. (Staff, 1987, p. 1-2)

By 1988, the comparison year used in this study, the members' profile survey form was changed to distinguish full- and part-time employment status. Only members who were working full time in 1988 and 1991 are included in this analysis of income. Part-time workers are excluded because they were likely to earn lower salaries by virtue of their part-time status and thus negatively affect aggregate incomes.

A large proportion of members did not respond to the question about their salaries. Only 41,300 members (40.9 percent of the data set of 100,899) reported their salaries from full-time employment in 1991, and 10,023 (11.6 percent of the data set of 86,091) did so for 1988.

NASW–RECOMMENDED SALARIES

In June 1990, the NASW Board of Directors adopted the following recommended minimum annual salaries for social workers: BSW, $20,000; MSW, $25,000; ACSW or MSW plus two years of social work experience, $30,000; and advanced professional—MSW plus special expertise at the administrative level—$45,000. NASW suggested that adjustments should be considered for the economic conditions of specific geographic areas. These standards may be compared to the actual salaries reported by NASW members in the two years.

PRIMARY INCOME

For both 1988 and 1991, the responses were slightly positively skewed (0.553 for 1988 and 0.391 for 1991), with the majority of respondents falling midway between low salaries (defined for the purposes of this discussion as below $15,000) and high salaries ($50,000 or more). The respondents' median range of income was $25,000–$29,999 in 1991 and $20,000–$24,999 in 1988 (see Figure 6.1).

In 1991, 44.3 percent (18,314) of the respondents earned less than $25,000, compared to 52.6 percent (5,276) in 1988—a modest decrease—and in 1991, 33.3 percent (13,753) earned $30,000 or more, compared to 24.2 percent (2,425) in 1988, a slightly higher proportion (see Table 6.1).

At the upper end of the income scale there was a modest gain. In 1988, 14.7 percent (1,470) of the respondents reported salaries of $35,000 or more, compared to 21.1 percent (8,721) in 1991; 2.6 percent (260) and 3.4 percent (1,404) reported salaries of $60,000 or more in 1988 and 1991, respectively.

At the lower income levels, 11.3 percent (1,129) of the 1988 respondents reported their salaries to be $17,499 or under versus 7.9 percent (3,278) of the 1991 respondents. The proportion of members reporting the lowest incomes did not decrease between 1988 and 1991. In 1988, 0.7 percent (69) of the respondents reported salaries of under $10,000, compared to 0.8 percent (329) in 1991.

Contrast these salaries with those reported in NASW's 1961 salary study (Becker, 1961). MSW graduates in the class of 1960 earned a median salary of $5,500. However, the real dollar value, as calculated by an inflator factor of 4.55 (the Consumer Price Index-U for 1961 was 29.9 and for 1991, 136.2) in 1991 dollars of those salaries is

FIGURE 6.1

Distribution of Primary Income of NASW Members, 1988 and 1991

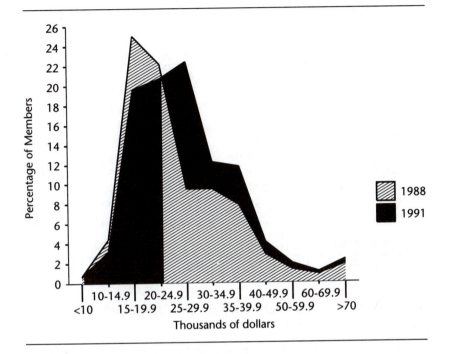

$25,025. Thus, the median income of NASW members has barely kept pace with inflation.

The relatively modest rate of growth in salaries among NASW members from 1988 to 1991 (see Table 6.2), however, was consistent with wider socioeconomic trends. The Economic Policy Institute ("Declining Wages," 1992) reported that 80 percent of the U.S. work force, including college graduates, white-collar workers, and most women, experienced substantial pay losses from 1987 to 1992, regardless of education.

Still, as the BLS (1991) reported, professional and technical workers in general received higher salaries than did NASW members in 1988 and 1991. In addition, the salaries of NASW members grew at a level equal to inflation, whereas other professionals experienced an increase in real income (see Table 6.3).

TABLE 6.1

Primary Income Comparisons of NASW Members Working Full Time: 1988 and 1991

Primary Income	1988		1991	
	n	%[a]	*n*	%
Under $10,000	69	0.7	329	0.8
$10,000–$14,499	445	4.4	1,324	3.2
$15,000–$19,999	2,520	25.1	8,098	19.6
$20,000–$24,999	2,242	22.4	8,563	20.7
$25,000–$29,999	2,322	23.2	9,233	22.4
$30,000–$34,999	955	9.5	5,032	12.2
$35,000–$39,999	796	7.9	4,829	11.7
$40,000–$49,999	279	2.8	1,709	4.1
$50,000–$59,999	135	1.3	779	1.9
$60,000 and over	260	2.6	1,404	3.4
Total respondents	10,023		41,300	

[a] Percentages do not total 100 because of rounding.

Primary Income, by the Highest Social Work Degree and Date of the Degree

As expected, those with advanced degrees earned higher salaries. In the 1991 data set, the largest proportion of BSW respondents—29.3 percent (681)—earned $17,600 to $19,999; the largest proportion of MSW respondents—23.4 percent (8,649)—earned $25,000 to

TABLE 6.2

Annual Primary Incomes, 1987 to 1991

Year	*n*	25th Percentile	Median	Mean	75th Percentile
1986–87	$26,338[a]	$22,500	$27,500	$27,800	$32,250
1988	10,100	18,749	22,499	26,617	27,499
1991	41,526	22,499	27,499	28,686	32,499

[a] The 1987 salary report (Staff, 1987) did not break out full- and part-time employment because this information was not available. Therefore, the 1987 figures are likely to be lower than if reported for only full-time incomes. Thus, the comparisons suggest, at best, that the full-time incomes of NASW members have not changed since 1988 and at worst that they have declined since 1988, particularly in relation to inflation.

TABLE 6.3

Income of NASW Members versus Other BLS Categories

Category	1988	1991	% Change
NASW members	$26,617	$28,686	7.8
BLS categories			
Professionals	45,088	51,359	13.9
Technical	30,756	33,487	8.9
Service	19,268	21,798	13.1
Construction	31,497	33,587	6.6
Machinists	26,507	28,692	8.2

Note: Source of BLS categories: Bureau of Labor Statistics (1991).

$29,999; and the largest proportion of PhD–DSW respondents—20.7 percent (348)—earned $35,000 to $39,000.

The income differentials by degree are most clearly evident at the upper and lower ranges. For example, 66.2 percent (1,541) of the BSW respondents earned $10,000 to $19,999, compared to 20.8 percent (7,706) of the MSW respondents and 5.1 percent (86) of the PhD–DSW respondents. At the other end of the income continuum, only 1.6 percent (39) of the BSW respondents versus 8.8 percent (3,270) of the MSW respondents and 32.9 percent (553) of the PhD–DSW respondents earned $40,000 or more (see Table 6.4).

As expected, the salaries were also positively associated with the date of receipt of the highest social work degree, that is, those who

TABLE 6.4

Primary Income of NASW Members, by Highest Social Work Degree, 1991

Primary Income	BSW	MSW[a]	PhD–DSW[a]
Under $10,000	3.7	0.6	0.5
$10,000–$19,999	66.2	20.8	5.1
$20,000–$29,999	22.7	45.0	26.1
$30,000–$39,999	5.8	24.6	35.3
Over $40,000	1.6	8.8	32.9
Total respondents	2,327	36,897	1,679
Percentage	5.7	90.2	4.1

[a] Percentages do not total 100 because of rounding.

obtained their degree earlier earned higher salaries (see Table 6.5). For example, of those who earned $60,000 to $69,000 in 1991, 30.6 percent (137) received their degree between 1961 and 1970 and 25.9 percent (116) received it between 1976 and 1980. On the other hand, less than 1 percent (64) of those who earned their highest degree after 1980 earned over $60,000 in 1991. At the lower income levels, only 0.3 percent (3) of those who received their highest degree between 1951 and 1960 earned $15,000 to $17,500, compared to 12 percent (202) of those who earned their degree after 1990.

The rate of increase appears to be more substantial for the first few years following graduation than for subsequent years. As Table 6.5 shows, salaries tend to rise more quickly during the first five years of practice. To achieve the same dollar growth experienced during the first five years of practice takes another 10 years. Income seems to level off after about 15 years after graduation; thereafter, there is relatively little difference in income related to the number of years out of school.

Primary Income, by Experience

Primary income is also positively correlated with years of experience; that is, the more experienced NASW members earn higher salaries. Of those earning $12,500 to $14,999 in 1991, 42.5 percent (199) had under two years of experience and 2.8 percent (13) had 26 or more years of experience. Only 5.6 percent (456) of the respondents with fewer than two years of experience earned $25,000 to $29,999 (the median range), compared with 23.9 percent (1,947) of those with six

TABLE 6.5

Primary Income of NASW Members, by Date of Highest Social Work Degree, 1951 to 1990

Date of Degree	Median	Mode	Midrange[a]
1951–60	$30,000–34,999	$35,000–39,999	$25,000–40,000
1961–70	30,000–34,999	35,000–39,999	25,000–40,000
1971–75	30,000–34,999	25,000–29,999	25,000–40,000
1976–80	25,000–29,999	25,000–29,999	20,000–35,999
1981–85	25,000–29,999	25,000–29,999	20,000–35,999
1986–90	20,000–24,999	15,000–19,999	17,500–24,999

[a] The midrange was calculated by excluding the highest 25 percent and the lowest 25 percent of reported salaries earned.

to 10 years of experience, and only 1 percent (8) of those earning
$70,000 or more had two to five years of experience, compared to
25.4 percent (213) who had 16 to 20 years of experience.

As with the date of receipt of the highest degree, an analysis of the
relationship between years of experience and primary income reveals a
delay in the growth of incomes for NASW members. Incomes increase
at a faster rate during the first five years of practice than they do
thereafter; this increase is followed by a 10-year plateau and then an
apparent stagnation in income after about 15 years (see Table 6.6).
Previous NASW salary studies (Becker, 1961; Staff, 1983, 1987) reported a similar finding; in all three studies, the plateau effect occurred
at the same time.

Primary Income, by Gender

As was discussed earlier, the median income of NASW members in
1991 ranged from $25,000 to $29,999. At the median, there was virtually the same proportion of male—22.6 percent (1,540)—and
female—22.0 percent (6,215)—respondents. This quick look hides the
significant gender-based differences in income for NASW members.
When gender is controlled, the median income of the female respondents was in the $17,500–$19,999 range and for the male respondents, in the $20,000–$24,999 range. The gender-based discrepancy in
income is further explicated by the modal range, which was $20,000
to $24,999 for the female respondents and $25,000 to $29,999 for the
male respondents.

As Table 6.7 indicates, the income range of proportionately more

TABLE 6.6

NASW Member Income by Years of Experience, 1991

Years of Experience	Median	Mode	Midrange[a]
Less than 2	$17,500–19,999	$17,500–19,999	$17,500–24,999
2–5	20,000–24,999	17,500–19,999	17,500–24,999
6–10	25,000–29,999	25,000–29,999	20,000–29,999
11–15	25,000–29,999	25,000–29,999	20,000–34,999
16–20	30,000–34,999	30,000–34,999	25,000–39,999
21–25	35,000–39,999	35,000–39,999	25,000–49,999
26 or more	30,000–34,999	35,000–39,000	25,000–39,999

[a] The midrange was calculated by excluding the highest 25 percent and the lowest 25
percent of reported salaries earned.

TABLE 6.7

Primary Income of NASW Members, by Gender, 1991

Primary Income	Female		Male	
	n	%	*n*	%
Less than $10,000	263	0.9	60	0.6
$10,000–$19,999	7,625	27.1	1,366	13.0
$20,000–$29,999	12,593	44.6	4,000	38.3
$30,000–$39,999	5,845	20.8	3,324	31.7
$40,000–$49,999	875	3.1	718	6.9
$50,000–$59,999	370	1.3	338	3.2
Over $60,000	619	2.2	661	6.3
Total respondents	28,190		10,467	

female respondents than male respondents was below the median, and the income range of a higher proportion of the male respondents than of the female respondents was above the median. This differential is accentuated by the fact that the NASW membership is overwhelmingly female.

These findings are consistent with other studies of gender-related differences in the income of social workers (Belon & Gould, 1977; Fanshel, 1976; Fortune & Hanks, 1988; Jennings & Daley, 1979; Strobino & McCoy, 1992; Sutton, 1982). *Salaries in Social Work* (Staff, 1987) reported that the male respondents earned, on average, about 30.5 percent more than did the female respondents. However, a caveat was noted regarding the impact of including part-time workers in the sample, since a higher proportion of female than male members are believed to work part time.

Various explanations have been offered for the inequities in the incomes of male and female social workers. One view is that men disproportionately hold administrative–management positions that pay higher salaries; this view received empirical support in chapter 5. It is also believed that men assume administrative positions earlier in their careers than do women and so earn higher salaries on the basis of the date of the degrees and years of experience (Belon & Gould, 1977; Jennings & Daley, 1979). Whatever the reason, the fact remains that male members earn significantly higher salaries than do female members.

Primary Income, by Ethnicity

Few differences were found in the primary income of NASW members by ethnicity, and those that were found were not statistically significant. There was a slight tendency for other Hispanics and Native Americans to earn lower salaries than members of other ethnic groups; thus, for example, in 1991, 2.9 percent (10) of the other Hispanic respondents earned $10,000 to $12,499, compared to 1.2 percent (27) of the African American respondents and 1.4 percent (429) of the white respondents.

At the highest income level ($70,000 or more), white and "other" respondents were disproportionately represented. For example, 2.3 percent (701) of the white respondents and 2.9 percent (13) of the "other" respondents earned $70,000 or more, in contrast to 1 percent (23) of the African American respondents and 1.2 percent (5) of the Chicano respondents. However, there was some variation by ethnicity within all the income ranges, but no consistent pattern.

Salaries in Social Work (Staff, 1987) revealed that African American members reported the highest mean salary, followed closely by members from the "other" category. In 1991, it was found that those in the "other" category had a slightly higher mean income ($29,843), followed by the Asian respondents ($29,431), the white respondents ($28,424), and the Puerto Rican respondents ($28,344) (see Table 6.8).

Primary Income, by Age

As was expected, the younger NASW respondents earned lower salaries than did the older NASW respondents. Of those earning $10,000 or less in 1991, 21 percent (65) were aged 21 to 25 and 8.7 percent (27) were aged 51 to 60. Similarly, of those earning $12,500 to $14,999, 24.4 percent (187) were aged 26 to 30 and 8.4 percent (64) were aged 46 to 50.

At the median-income range of $25,000 to $29,999, 1.1 percent (96) were aged 21 to 25 and 22 percent (1,882) were aged 41 to 45. Only three respondents aged 30 or under reported annual salaries of $60,000 or more. The higher the income category, the higher the proportion of older members.

As Table 6.9 indicates, 84.1 percent of the respondents were aged 30 to 59 in 1991, compared to 84.7 percent in 1987. Although the average primary income was higher for each successive age group, the increments and the midrange tended to remain constant. This finding

TABLE 6.8

Annual Primary Income of NASW Members, by Ethnicity, 1991

| Ethnicity | n | % of Total | Annual Primary Income | | | |
			25th Percentile	Median	Mean	75th Percentile
White	30,853	87.0	$18,749	$27,499	$28,424	$32,499
African American	2,311	6.5	22,499	27,499	28,267	32,499
Asian	549	1.5	22,499	29,999	29,431	32,499
Puerto Rican	324	0.9	22,499	27,499	28,344	32,499
Chicano	414	1.2	22,499	27,499	28,238	32,499
Other Hispanic	349	1.0	18,749	27,499	26,729	32,499
Native American	214	0.6	18,749	22,499	26,306	32,499
Other	456	1.3	22,499	29,999	29,843	32,499
Total respondents	35,470					

TABLE 6.9

Annual Primary Income of NASW Members, by Age, 1991

Age	n	% of Total	Annual Primary Income			
			25th Percentile	Median	Mean	75th Percentile
Under 30	4,698	12.3	$16,249	$18,749	$20,009	$22,499
30–39	12,337	32.2	18,749	22,499	25,987	27,499
40–49	13,954	36.5	22,499	27,499	29,788	32,499
50–59	5,911	15.4	22,499	27,499	32,622	37,499
60 and over	1,402	3.6	22,499	32,499	33,222	37,499
Total respondents	38,302					

is consistent with the findings presented earlier that the salaries of members are in three stages, with a plateau after the fifth and tenth years of practice.

Primary Income, by Primary Practice Area

Salaries in Social Work (Staff, 1987, p. 9) identified the primary area of practice as "probably the most representative of how social workers view themselves and how they are identified by the public." At that time, 33.1 percent of the sample identified themselves as providing mental health services and having a mean income of $29,000. The situation remained relatively constant from 1987 to 1991, when 30.8 percent of the respondents reported the same primary area of practice, with a mean primary income of $31,480.

An analysis of the 1991 primary income by primary practice area shows that the median and mean salaries of the respondents fell within a narrow range: $22,499 to $33,516. However, there was a discernible trend in this midrange income by primary areas of practice. As Table 6.10 indicates, the midrange incomes of three basic groups of primary practice areas differed. Those with primary practice areas in services to the aged, mentally retarded–developmentally disabled, and persons with other disabilities earned $22,499 to $27,499, with a midrange of $24,332 to $25,923. The midrange income of respondents whose primary practice areas were children, families, medical clinics, substance abuse, school social work, and corrections was $22,499 to $32,499, with a mean range of $26,834 to $28,855. The highest income-producing areas of social work practice appear to be public assistance, occupational social work, mental health, community organization–planning, and group services. The midrange for this group was from $27,499 to $37,499, with a mean income of $29,365 to $33,516. However, except for mental health services, these primary practice areas represent less than 10 percent of the respondents who were working full time.

As Figure 6.2 illustrates, those reporting the highest incomes ($70,000 or more) were concentrated in three primary practice areas: group services (6.3 percent), community organization–planning (5.8 percent), and mental health services (4.4 percent). In contrast, those reporting the lowest incomes (below $10,000) were in services to the disabled (3.1 percent), occupational social work (2.9 percent), and community organization–planning (2.3 percent).

TABLE 6.10

Annual Primary Income of NASW Members, by Primary Practice Area, 1991

Primary Practice Area	n	% of Total	Annual Primary Income			
			25th Percentile	Median	Mean	75th Percentile
Aged	1,901	4.7	$18,748	$22,499	$24,332	$27,499
Other disabilities	237	0.6	18,749	22,499	25,869	27,499
Mental retardation–developmental disabilities	1,268	3.1	18,749	22,499	25,923	27,499
Children's services	7,056	17.4	18,749	22,499	26,834	32,499
Family services	4,151	10.2	18,749	22,499	27,034	32,499
Medical clinics	5,316	13.1	22,499	27,499	27,141	32,499
Substance abuse	1,980	4.9	18,749	22,499	27,517	32,499
School social work	2,086	5.1	22,499	27,499	28,678	32,499
Corrections	539	1.3	22,499	27,499	28,855	32,499
Public assistance	410	1.0	18,749	27,499	29,365	37,499
Occupational social work	344	0.8	22,499	27,499	29,866	32,499
Combined areas	2,302	5.7	18,749	27,499	30,367	32,499
Mental health	12,506	30.8	22,499	27,499	31,480	37,499
Community organization–planning	398	1.0	22,499	27,499	32,175	37,499
Group services	174	0.4	22,499	27,499	33,516	37,499
Total respondents	40,668					

FIGURE 6.2

Percentage of NASW Members Reporting High and Low Incomes, by Primary Area of Practice, 1991

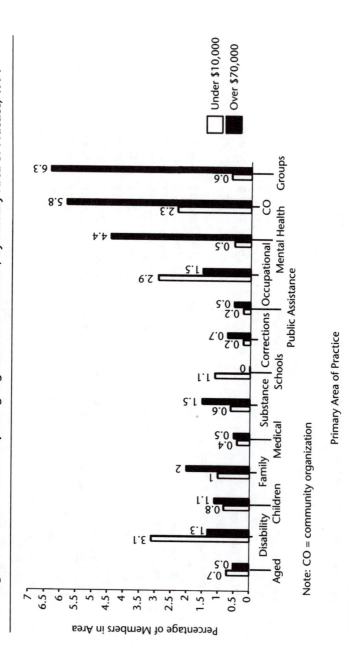

Note: CO = community organization

Primary Income, by Primary Setting

The midrange incomes for 1991 fell into five categories, according to the primary settings in which the respondents practiced (see Table 6.11). The low midrange category ($16,249 to $27,499, with a median of $18,749) consisted of respondents employed in group homes and nursing homes. One explanation for the low income in these settings is that the workers tend to be newer graduates with lesser degrees (BSWs rather than MSWs) than those in other settings.

The respondents in the second midrange category ($18,749 to $27,499) were employed in clinics (mean = $26,057), agencies (mean = $26,185), institutions (mean = $26,988), and hospitals (mean = $27,125). The third category ($22,499 to $32,499) comprised respondents who worked in the schools (mean = $28,615) and courts (mean = $28,651).

The fourth category ($22,499 to $37,499) consisted of respondents who were employed in membership organizations, non–social work settings, and universities. The mean primary incomes for this category (membership organizations, $31,072; non–social work settings, $31,259; and universities, $32, 021) were above the median ($27,499) and mean ($28,686) for the total membership in 1991 (see Table 6.2).

The fifth category ($22,499 to $54,999) comprised respondents who were in private practice—both private group and private solo. The median and mean incomes of these respondents were significantly above those of the membership as a whole: private group—median income = $32,499, with a mean of $38,413—and private solo—median = $37,399, with a mean of $45,271. Although this difference from the median for the entire membership may be significant, it is not clear whether the gross or net income was reported. If the gross income was reported, it was offset by the cost of office space and employee benefits (health insurance, retirement, life insurance, and professional liability coverage) that are often included as fringe benefits in other settings. Such deductions from gross income could reduce the net yearly income for private practitioners to an amount equal to or below the median of the overall membership who were working full time.

Nevertheless, as Figure 6.3 shows, the proportion of members who reported higher income ranges in 1991 differed significantly according to the settings in which they practiced. A substantially higher percentage of the respondents in private solo and private group settings reported incomes over $60,000 (24.5 and 13.5 percent, respectively).

TABLE 6.11

Annual Primary Income of NASW Members, by Primary Setting, 1991

Primary Setting	n	% of Total	Annual Primary Income			
			25th Percentile	Median	Mean	75th Percentile
Group home	1,071	2.6	$16,249	$18,749	$22,105	$27,499
Nursing home	1,026	2.5	16,249	18,749	22,664	27,499
Clinic	7,194	17.8	18,749	22,499	26,057	27,499
Agency	9,838	24.3	18,749	22,499	26,185	32,499
Institution	1,335	3.3	18,749	22,499	26,988	27,499
Hospital	9,473	3.3	18,749	22,499	27,125	27,499
School	2,706	6.7	22,499	27,499	28,615	32,499
Court	659	1.6	22,499	27,499	28.651	32,499
Membership organization	278	0.7	22,499	27,499	31,072	37,499
Non–social work setting	813	2.0	22,499	27,499	31,259	37,499
University	1,568	3.9	22,499	27,499	32,021	37,499
Private group practice	1,340	3.3	22,499	32,499	38,413	44,999
Private solo practice	3,194	7.9	27,499	37,499	45,271	54,999
Total respondents	40,495					

FIGURE 6.3

Percentage of NASW Members Reporting High and Low Incomes, by Primary Practice Setting, 1991

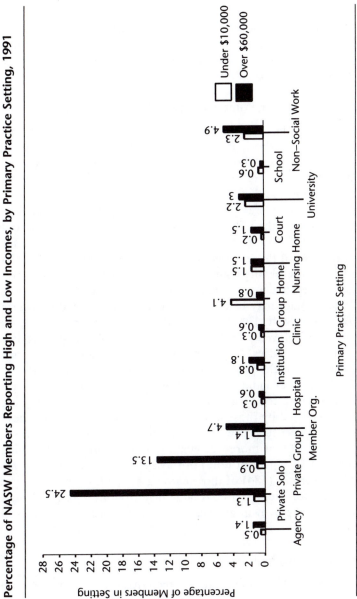

The next highest proportions of respondents in this income range were in non–social work settings (4.9 percent), membership organizations (4.7 percent), and group homes (4.1 percent). It is interesting that the respondents in these same settings also reported the highest percentage of incomes below $10,000.

Primary Income, by Primary Auspice of Employment

In 1991, the salaries of respondents in the public sector were, in general, higher than those of respondents in the private not-for-profit sector. Furthermore, those who worked for the federal government or military earned higher salaries than did those who worked for local or state governments. For example, 24 percent (295) of those who worked for the federal government and 24.1 percent (84) of those who worked for the military earned $30,000 to $34,999, but only 13.4 percent (1,063) of those employed by local governments and 14.7 percent (926) of those employed by state governments earned that amount. However, the highest incomes ($27,499 to $37,499) were reported by respondents in the private for-profit sector.

These findings may be compared with those reported in *Salaries in Social Work* (Staff, 1987). For the 1986–87 membership year, the respondents employed in military and federal public service reported the highest mean salaries. In contrast, the highest mean reported income in 1991 was for the private for-profit sector (see Table 6.12).

The largest percentage of NASW members employed by the private not-for-profit sector earned $17,500 to $29,999, with slightly higher salaries reported by those in nonsectarian not-for-profit agencies than in sectarian agencies. The largest proportion of NASW members earning $40,000 or more was employed in the private for-profit sector, and 62.1 percent (266) of those earning $60,000 to $69,000 and 78.2 percent (684) of those earning $70,000 or more worked in the private for-profit sector. A large majority of the respondents who listed their employment auspice as private for-profit were probably self-employed.

Primary Income, by Primary Function

From 1986 to 1991, the mean income range by function remained stagnant, but the functions shifted rank in relation to each other. In 1991, the respondents with the primary functions of planning, direct service, or non–social work reported lower incomes than did those with primary functions in policy, consultation, and management (see

120

TABLE 6.12

Annual Primary Income of NASW Members, by Primary Auspice, 1991

Primary Auspice	n	% of Total	Annual Primary Income			
			25th Percentile	Median	Mean	75th Percentile
Private not-for-profit sectarian	4,783	12.3	$18,749	$22,499	$25,328	$27,499
Private not-for-profit nonsectarian	10,583	27.2	18,749	22,499	26,500	27,499
Public local	7,925	20.4	18,749	27,499	27,342	32,499
Public state	6,294	16.2	22,499	27,499	28,215	32,499
Public federal	1,229	3.2	22,499	27,499	29,721	32,499
Military	349	0.9	22,499	27,499	29,853	32,499
Private for-profit	7,681	19.8	22,499	27,499	35,458	37,499
Total respondents	38,844					

Table 6.13). Midway on the income continuum were those with primary functions in supervision, education, and research. In contrast, in *Salaries in Social Work* (Staff, 1987), the lowest incomes were for those in direct service, consultation, and planning; the highest incomes were for those in management, education, and supervision; and the midrange incomes were for those in research.

The midrange salaries for those in direct service, planning, and non-social work primary functions were $18,749 to $27,499; for those in supervision, $22,499 to $32,499; and for those in consultation, $22,499 to $37,999. The midrange salaries of those in management were $22,499 to $37,499, with, as is discussed later, a significant number earning salaries at the upper end of the continuum, and the midrange salaries of those in both education and policy were $22,499 to $37,499.

These findings are consistent with those of earlier NASW salary studies and with the literature pertaining to salary equity in the profession. *Salaries in Social Work* (Staff, 1987) found that the highest mean salary (then $35,200) was earned by those in management and administration and the lowest mean salary by those in direct service (then $25,300).

The primary functions of consultation (6.9 percent), research (5.8 percent), and non–social work (5.8 percent) had the highest proportion of respondents who reported incomes over $60,000 (see Figure 6.4). However, direct service, management, and education had the largest percentages of those reporting the highest levels of primary income. Of those reporting incomes of $60,000 to $69,000, 59.9 percent (278) were in direct service, and of those reporting incomes of $70,000 or more, 74 percent (677) were in direct service. Findings related to primary income by primary setting (discussed earlier) suggest that these high-income earners were in private solo or group practice.

The second largest proportion of members earning over $60,000 were in management (4.1 percent) and direct service (3.5 percent). Others with this income level were in planning (2.3 percent), policy (2.2 percent), and education (2 percent).

Primary Income, by Region

There are discernible variations in income, depending on the region of the country in which members practice. Members who reside in the New England, Mid-Atlantic, South Atlantic, and Pacific states are more likely to earn higher salaries. For example, in 1991, of those

TABLE 6.13

Annual Primary Income of NASW Members, by Primary Function, 1991

Primary Function	n	% of Total	Annual Primary Income			
			25th Percentile	Median	Mean	75th Percentile
Planning	129	0.3	$18,749	$22,499	$26,309	$27,499
Direct service	27,273	66.8	18,749	22,499	26,993	27,499
Non–social work	447	1.1	16,249	22,499	27,726	32,499
Supervision	2,977	7.3	22,499	27,499	28,276	32,499
Research	136	0.3	22,499	27,499	30,365	32,499
Education	1,618	4.0	22,499	27,499	31,204	37,499
Policy	223	0.5	22,499	32,499	32,053	37,499
Consultation	392	1.0	22,499	27,499	32,326	37,499
Management	7,607	18.6	22,499	32,499	34,112	37,499
Total respondents	40,802					

FIGURE 6.4

Percentage of NASW Members Reporting High and Low Incomes, by Primary Function, 1991

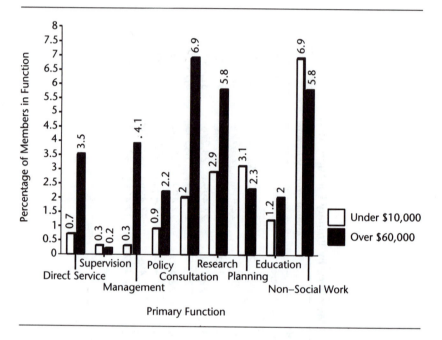

earning $60,000 to $69,999, 28.2 percent (131) lived in the Mid-Atlantic states, 17 percent (79) lived in the South Atlantic states, and 16.3 (76) lived in the Pacific states. Of those earning $70,000 or more, 30 percent (277) lived in the Mid-Atlantic states, 15.3 (141) lived in the South Atlantic states, and 17.7 (164) lived in the Pacific states. The proportion of respondents who earned incomes below the median of $25,000 to $29,999 in these three regions was also lower than the proportion of members earning low incomes in other regions. Incomes tended to be lower for those in the East South Central region, followed by the West South Central region (see Table 6.14).

SECONDARY INCOME

The income from secondary employment earned by NASW members employed full time was low in both 1988 and 1991, and the over-

124

TABLE 6.14

Annual Primary Income of NASW Members, by Region, 1991

Region	n	% of Total	Annual Primary Income			
			25th Percentile	Median	Mean	75th Percentile
Territories	33	0.1	$13,749	$22,499	$23,302	$27,499
East South Central	1,388	3.4	16,249	22,499	24,480	27,499
West North Central	2,784	6.8	18,749	22,499	26,067	27,499
East North Central	7,844	19.0	18,749	22,499	27,069	27,499
West South Central	2,859	6.9	18,749	22,499	27,462	27,499
Mountain	1,848	4.5	18,749	27,499	28,001	32,499
South Atlantic	6,035	14.7	18,749	27,499	28,494	32,499
New England	3,906	9.5	18,749	27,499	29,063	32,499
Mid-Atlantic	9,544	23.2	22,499	27,499	30,411	32,499
Pacific	4,937	12.0	13,749	27,499	31,323	32,499
Total respondents	41,178					

whelming majority of members did not report any secondary income in those years. (This finding may reflect the failure to complete the renewal questionnaire more than the absence of a secondary income.) Of the 2,184 respondents who reported a secondary income in 1988, 69.1 percent (1,509) earned under $5,000 from that source, and only 6.7 percent (147) reported a secondary income of $15,000 or more. The proportions were similar for the 12,169 respondents in 1991: 66.8 percent (8,126) earned $4,999 or less, and 7.8 percent (950) earned $15,000 or more—a modest proportional increase over 1988.

Income from secondary sources has, however, risen over time. In 1961, less than 10 percent of the NASW membership received remuneration from more than one job (Becker, 1961, p. 3). This proportion had risen to 21.8 percent (2,184) of the 10,023 data set in 1988, and 29.5 percent (12,169) of the 41,300 data set in 1991. Of those reporting a secondary income in 1991, 58.9 percent (4,795) worked in the private for-profit sector and 46.9 percent (4,786) engaged in direct service as their secondary function. These data suggest that the majority of NASW members who earn a secondary income do so in private solo or group practice.

CHAPTER HIGHLIGHTS

- The midrange of the primary income reported by NASW members working full time was $20,000 to $24,000, and the median income was $25,000 to $30,000.

- Compared to the income reported in the 1961 salary study, income reported by members in 1991 had just kept pace with inflation.

- The increase in salaries from 1987 to 1991 was less than the rate of inflation.

- In 1991, the salaries reported by NASW members were significantly lower than those reported by others employed in professional and technical positions in the country, and the primary incomes of members are growing at a slower rate than those of their professional and technical counterparts.

- The primary income of the members is affected by their highest social work degree, date of degree, and time since receiving the degree.

- Reported incomes rise faster during the first five years of practice than thereafter. Also, NASW members appear to reach an income plateau after about 10 years of practice, after which increases in income are negligible.

- There is evidence of a significant gender bias in the incomes reported by the members: men earn more and are disproportionately overrepresented at the higher end of the income range and women are disproportionately overrepresented at the lower end.

- Those working in settings related to the aged and disabled (such as group homes and nursing homes) reported incomes at the low end of the income range in both years, whereas those working in settings related to mental health, community organization–planning, and group services reported incomes at the high end.

- Those working in private practice reported the highest mean and ceiling incomes, but their incomes may not include adjustments for overhead and employee benefits.

- Except for workers in private practice, governmental workers reported higher incomes than did nongovernmental workers.

- Members who worked in the New England, Mid-Atlantic, and Pacific regions reported higher incomes, and those who worked in the U.S. territories and in the East South Central and West North Central regions reported lower incomes than did those in other regions of the country.

REFERENCES

Becker, R. (1961). *Study of salaries of NASW members*. New York: National Association of Social Workers.

Belon, C. J., & Gould, K. H. (1977). Not even equals: Sex-related inequities. *Social Work, 22*, 466-471.

Bureau of Labor Statistics. (1991). *Household data survey: Employed civilians by detailed occupation, 1983–1991*. Washington, DC: Author.

Declining wages for high school and college graduates. (1992, July 12). *Washington Post*, p. H2.

Fanshel, D. (1976). Status differentials: Men and women in social work. *Social Work, 21*, 448-455.

Fortune, A. E., & Hanks, L. L. (1988). Gender inequities in early social work careers. *Social Work, 33*, 221-226.

Jennings, P. L., & Daley, M. (1979). Sex discrimination in social work careers. *Social Work Research & Abstracts, 15*, 17–21.

Staff. (1983, November). Membership survey shows practice shifts. *NASW News*, pp. 6–7.

Staff. (1987). *Salaries in social work: A summary report on the salaries of NASW members, July 1986–June 1987.* Silver Spring, MD: National Association of Social Workers.

Strobino, J., & McCoy, M. (1992). Recruitment, retention and promotion: Management issues related to salary equity. In Lynne M. Healy and Barbara A. Pine (Eds.), *Managers' choices* (pp. 27–43). Boca Raton, FL: National Network for Social Work Managers.

Sutton, J. A. (1982). Sex discrimination among social workers. *Social Work, 27*, 211–217.

CHAPTER 7

WHERE WE ARE GOING

TRENDS AND ISSUES

The findings presented in this volume allow for the identification of a number of trends and issues regarding the composition of the profession, the scope of the members' professional roles, and changes in the nature of practice. This chapter discusses some of these trends and issues and their implications for the profession and for NASW.

FEMINIZATION OF THE PROFESSION

The proportion of female NASW members rose from 68 percent in 1961 (Becker, 1961, p. 3), to 73 percent in 1982, to 74 percent in 1986 (Staff, 1987, p. 4), to 74.9 percent in 1988, and to 77.3 percent in 1991. Thus, the trend toward an increasing proportion of women in the NASW membership has been consistent and is growing.

The trend is mirrored among the larger population of social workers. The proportion of all social work positions held by women was 57 percent in 1960 (BLS, 1961), 64 percent in 1983, 65 percent in 1987, and 68 percent in 1991 (BLS, 1991).

The issue is not that social work as a profession and NASW as a professional association are dominated by women, but the impact of this female domination on the profession in light of this society's devaluation of women, their role in society, and their professional contributions. Historically, the effects of these societal biases have been observed in female-dominated professions, including teaching and nursing (Etzioni, 1969). Women, and the professions they dominate, have received lower salaries and been held in less social esteem than have men and the professions they dominate.

Despite the advances made in teaching and nursing, salary disparities by gender and profession, described next, continue to be an issue for the profession and for NASW and its members. Similarly, the tendency for male NASW members to hold proportionately more management positions raises serious questions of equity and parity in the profession.

YOUTH AND INEXPERIENCE OF THE MEMBERSHIP

The median age range of NASW members, for both 1988 and 1991, was 41 to 45. The proportion of members aged 51 and over decreased from 1988 to 1991, whereas the proportion of members under age 30 increased significantly.

Trends in social work education offer one explanation for the large and growing proportion of younger NASW members. These trends include the decline in the number of full-time degree students but a dramatic increase in the number of part-time degree students, the increased demand for off-campus and extension programs, and the proliferation of graduate and undergraduate programs (Bernard, 1987). The latter, it can be assumed, would not occur if there was not an actual or potential student market.

NASW has taken active steps to recruit new members from among the student population. Twice a year, it distributes promotional information to all graduate and undergraduate social work education programs to encourage students to join the association. In addition, the membership fee for students is discounted because NASW considers the recruitment of students to be an investment in the future. The rationale is clear, but the results are less certain.

In 1988, 12.8 percent (14,776) of the total NASW membership (116,296) consisted of individuals reporting student status. Despite intensive recruitment efforts, this proportion remained unchanged in 1991. Still, the number of student members (17,083 of 134,240) did rise. Furthermore, the recent graduates who joined NASW in these two years were younger than those who joined earlier in the association's history.

Age usually reflects experience, but not among the NASW members. Perhaps because of career shifts or the patterns of professional education that are consistent with a female-dominated profession, NASW members tend to complete their highest professional degrees later in life than do people in other professions. Consequently, the members' level of experience is not necessarily what their ages would suggest.

From 1988 to 1991, the proportion of members with fewer than two years of experience rose dramatically, whereas the proportion of members with more than 10 years of experience fell considerably.

CSWE (Spaulding, 1991) reported that enrollments in accredited social work degree granting programs are on the increase. Traditionally, one effect of downturns in the economy is that students stay in school longer and go on to graduate school sooner after they complete their undergraduate degrees. Thus, the shifts in the age and experience of NASW members between 1988 and 1991 may have been due to anomalies in higher education as a result of recent economic downturns.

Another explanation for the growing proportion of young NASW members has to do with the retention of members. The proportion of younger members may be just as much a reflection of the decrease in older members through attrition than to trends in the educational system. If this speculation is true, the question is whether this attrition is due to (1) the natural aging of the membership, or (2) the abandonment of the profession by older members, who may seek more lucrative employment in other professions. A third possibility is that some members cease to consider NASW membership relevant to their needs and interests as they progress in their careers. Whatever the basis of the phenomenon, it is of utmost importance to NASW and the professionals it represents. Clearly, studies on lapsed members are necessary.

MULTICULTURAL CHARACTERISTICS

Social work is standing still, if not falling back, in its efforts to attract ethnically diverse populations to the profession. There was a steady decline in the proportion of minorities among MSW students from 1969 to 1987—from 21.6 percent of the full-time students (CSWE, 1969) to 13.9 percent (Spaulding, 1991). Although the trend seems to be reversing, students from ethnic minority populations received only 15.9 percent of the MSW degrees awarded in 1990 (Spaulding, 1991). At the same time, the BLS (1991) reported an increase in the proportion of minorities in social work positions nationwide. In 1991, 29.1 percent of all those holding social work positions were African American or Hispanic (the only two ethnic minority groups for which statistics are reported), compared to 23.3 percent in 1984.

The two primary issues for the profession in this regard are the underrepresentation of people of color in social work and the lower proportion of NASW members of color compared to their numbers in the social services labor force.

The recruitment of people of color into the profession has been less successful than in earlier years, primarily because of the increased openness and accessibility of other professions to ethnic minorities. With these increased opportunities, it may be surmised that people of color are choosing careers in other, often more lucrative, fields. A compounding factor is social work's decreased emphasis on advocacy. Williams (1987, p. 344) supported this view:

> Trends since the mid-1970s suggest that the profession will do even less for these [minority] groups as resources grow more scarce and as schools of social work gear up to respond to the needs of a current wave of recruits who are interested in family counseling and individual psychotherapy. These recruits indicate a distaste for advocacy and for the case management and resource provision skills that are traditional in working with disadvantaged groups and minorities.

Given the number of professional organizations and special-interest groups that have a direct bearing on the practice of social work, it is probable that many NASW members belong to more than one association. Williams (1987, pp. 341–342) noted that many NASW members

> also belong to specialized function associations or to other organizations that, in most instances, complement and further the services and objectives of NASW. (In some cases, however, other organizations may exist as challenges to NASW objectives.)

The parenthetical comment about potential competitors of NASW may explain why some people of color do not join NASW.

Special-interest associations are basically of two types: (1) those having a racial, religious, or ethnic identity and (2) those representing specialized functions (Williams, 1987, p. 342). Among the former groups are the National Association of Black Social Workers (NABSW) and the National Association of Puerto Rican Social Service Workers (NAPRSW). Associations representing specialized functions include the National Federation of Societies for Clinical Social Work and the American Association for Marriage and Family Therapy. Specialty groups that have both an institutional and individual membership include the Child Welfare League of America and the American Public Welfare Association.

It is not known whether people of color do not join NASW because they join other associations, if they join both NASW and other associations, or if they simply do not join any association. But the number of members of NABSW suggests that many join an association other than, rather than in addition to, NASW. The membership of NABSW was over 10,000 in 1987 (Williams, 1987, p. 344), significantly higher than the 6,690 African American members of NASW in 1991.

WITHDRAWAL FROM PUBLIC SERVICE ROLE

In 1961, government at the federal, state, or municipal level was the major employer of NASW members. The 1961 salary study (Becker, 1961, p. 5) found that "contrary to the long-held belief that the most highly trained social workers tend not to favor employment in the public services, the survey of NASW members shows that more than 52 percent work for federal, state, county, and municipal governmental agencies."

From 1961 to 1991, this situation changed significantly. Declassification (the reduction in standards of professional education and work-related experience for public social service jobs) has been a formidable challenge to the profession (Pecora & Austin, 1983, p. 421). In 1981, the NASW Delegate Assembly adopted a policy statement on declassification ("Declassification," 1988, p. 155) that noted

> public social service departments have failed to recognize the profession of social work as a major contributor to effective social services and advocacy for the welfare movement in this country. This lack of recognition is evident in the trend toward eliminating social workers from policymaking, supervision, and direct services.

Among the reasons cited for this state of affairs were

- the unavailability of BSWs and MSWs, due to disinterest or too few numbers, to fill the positions needed to expand the staffing of public programs
- the assumption that on-the-job training could and would compensate for professionally earned social work degrees
- the tendency of unions, representing state, county, and municipal employees, to promote on the basis of agency experience rather than professional education
- the emphasis on quantitative rather than qualitative accountability among public agencies
- the undifferentiated use of BSWs and MSWs, resulting in the assumption that a master's degree is superfluous to service provision

- the proliferation of legislation and administrative rules that allow equivalences to social work education
- the lowering of standards for hiring due to dwindling resources ("Declassification," 1988, p. 155).

These factors have resulted in a redefinition of functions associated with the provision of public social services in a manner that is no longer congruent with social work practice.

Moreover, the phenomenon of declassification may include a "backlash" against social workers. Disenchantment with the social advocacy movement of the 1960s, spiraling public welfare and social service costs attributed to the War on Poverty, and the passage of Medicare and Medicaid and other (liberal) changes in entitlement programs were contributors to the conservatism of the 1970s and 1980s and the removal of public welfare from the domain of social workers. Walz and Groze (1991) noted that during the 1970s professional social workers were transferred from management and policy positions to service units or other positions in which they would have a limited influence on policy. These changes, they contended, resulted in social work's virtual abandonment of public welfare.

Cutbacks in federal funds for training, which supported many public welfare employees through MSW programs during the 1960s, also had an impact on the number of graduates entering or returning to public social service employment (Gibelman, 1983). Meanwhile, other social work specialties, primarily the private practice of social work, were gaining ground. The growth in private practice was also attributable to external forces, such as third-party vendorship, made possible by the increased number of states offering licensure to social workers. Thus, the role of NASW members in public social services was affected by the deemphasis on social work intervention in the public sector and the concurrent increase of professional opportunities in the for-profit sector. These shifts had the longer-term effect of altering the demographics of the clientele with whom NASW members and other social workers traditionally worked—the poor and disenfranchised.

INCREASE IN PRIVATE PRACTICE

Social work has traditionally been practiced in organizational settings. The history of the profession has been marked by a consistent and dual tension between a focus on the individual and a focus on the environment. This dynamic tension can be construed, in terms of practice, as a blend of functions that focus on individuals and on advocacy. Hopps and Pinderhughes (1987, p. 353), however, noted that the tension often reaches such levels that choices must be made:

> The profession is anchored on one side by service to and empowerment of those in acute need, and on the other by the dominant segment of society that controls the resources and sharing of power essential to meeting that need.
>
> In its more expansive cycles, society tends to view social work as a mirror of its own openhandedness and optimism. However, in times of stasis, contrived shortage, or divisiveness . . . the values and practitioners of social work become unwelcome reflections on societal priorities and injustices. At such times, the profession's members face difficult choices about the extent to which they serve as arms of the institutional structures or as advocates of the excluded. Consequently, more than any other profession, social work tends to be vulnerable to shifts in the social climate. The profession's fluctuating emphases on cause and function and on environmental reform and individual change have all reflected the boundaries of the profession and its responsiveness to milieu.

One means of resolving the tension between institutional structures and their constraints and commitment to serving human needs may be evident in the trend toward independent practice. The data reveal that private practice has become an increasingly important alternative for the provision of social work services. In private or proprietary practice, the social worker is employed directly by the client and is paid by the client, either directly or through a vendorship arrangement. The private practitioners usually provide for their own offices, personnel benefits, staff support, record keeping, and so forth (Barker, 1987, p. 324).

Barker (1984, p. 20) defined the private practice of social work as

> the process in which the values, knowledge, and skills of social work, which were acquired through sufficient education and experience, are used to deliver social services autonomously to clients in exchange for mutually agreed payment.

The distinctions between private and agency practice include

- The social worker is employed by and obligated to his or her clients rather than the employing agency.
- The social worker determines which clients he or she will see rather than agency supervisors or administrators assigning cases.

- The social worker determines the focus and method of intervention or treatment. If consultation on a case is sought, including the type of intervention, it is at the discretion of the private practitioner. In an agency, case conferences with a supervisor are generally part of everyday practice.
- There is no predetermined and fixed salary. In private practice, the social worker receives fees for specific services directly from the client or on behalf of the client (in the case of vendorship) (Barker, 1987).

The proportion of NASW members engaged in private practice has steadily increased. Disillusionment with agency-based practice, economic need, desire to gain control over working conditions, and interest in concentrating on clinical work with particular populations or types of presenting problems have been cited as some of the motivating reasons for the growth in private practice (Abramovitz, 1986; Jayaratne, Davis-Sacks, & Chess, 1991; Saxton, 1988). NASW's studies reveal that the proportion of members engaged in private practice increased from 10.9 percent in 1982 to 15.3 percent in 1987 (Staff, 1987). Unfortunately, these data do not differentiate between primary and secondary practice or between solo and group private practice. By 1988, the proportion of NASW members in private solo and group primary practice was 13.1 percent and in secondary practice, 41.7 percent. In 1991, 15 percent of NASW members cited private solo and group as their primary areas of practice and 42.7 cited them as their secondary areas.

Although the merits and pitfalls of the private practice of social work have been debated for years, the debate should now logically focus on the following implications of private practice:

- The consequences of private practice on the profession and for the delivery of services: who gets served, with what types of interventions, for how long, and with what outcomes.
- The career paths, salaries, and demographics of private practitioners compared to other social workers.
- As private practice takes on a distinctly individual-oriented nature, how does the profession reconcile its role in and commitment to the development of social policy and the management of the service delivery system?
- How do private practitioners honor a professional code of ethics that not only requires services to individuals, but delineates social

workers' responsibility to make larger social systems more responsive to the needs of individuals?

MACRO–LEVEL SOCIAL WORK PRACTICE

The proportion of NASW members whose positions involve the primary or secondary functions of policy, consultation, research, or planning is negligible. And although management is better represented as a primary function among the members than are the other macro areas of practice, less than 20 percent of the members' primary or secondary functions are in management. These findings contradict the traditional wisdom about the extent of vertical and horizontal mobility in the profession.

One explanation for these data may be simply that social workers in macro practice do not join NASW or let their membership lapse because they think that membership in NASW is not relevant to their work or that another association represents their interests better. Another explanation may be that only a small proportion of all social workers perform policy, planning, consultation, or research functions and hold such positions. Supporting this latter view is the increasing trend of public and not-for-profit social service agencies to hire people trained in business and public administration for management. A third explanation may be that, either by choice or because of shifts in the job market, the movement to private practice is focused more on interventions at the individual level than at the macro level.

DEVIATION FROM NASW'S RECOMMENDED SALARIES

The salaries reported by NASW members who were employed full time in both 1988 and 1991 fell short of the levels recommended by NASW. However, this deviation has historical roots. The 1961 NASW salary study (Becker, 1961, p. 4) reported that "the worker with ten to fifteen years of experience is earning a median salary of $7,500— considerably less than the goal of $10,000 set by NASW salary standards for experienced and competent workers with ten years of experience."

Salaries have remained stagnant. It should be recalled that the 1961 and 1991 median salaries of NASW members were virtually identical when adjusted for inflation. In the years immediately following the creation of NASW in 1955, the association focused on attracting and maintaining members "through an appeal to their need for status and improved salaries" (Beck, 1977, p. 1090). In 1957, NASW began its periodic publication of minimum salary standards (Battle, 1987). Social workers' low pay has been a longstanding concern and has been the object of strategic planning by NASW since the association's inception. It remains a major item on NASW's agenda.

Beyond the generally lower-than-average professional salaries of NASW members is the internal issue of gender-based bias in the members' incomes. In 1961, 32 percent of the members were male and earned a median salary of $7,700, compared to the female members' median salary of $6,600 (Becker, 1961, p. 4). The 1986–87 salary study (Staff, 1987, p. 4) revealed that, on average, the male respondents earned about 30.5 percent more than did the female respondents. These disparities held true for the 1988 and 1991 membership. In fact, an analysis of variance of primary income by gender for 1991, controlling for experience, degree, and function, indicated that gender was a significant factor in the variances in income. As much as 24 percent of the differential in primary income, with men earning more, could be accounted for by gender. In a stepwise multiple regression, gender accounted for more of the differential in primary income than did auspice, setting, practice, or function.

CHANGING VOCABULARY

Casework has traditionally been the predominant method of social work practice. But in 1980, the question was raised, "What is clinical social work?" It was noted that the term *clinical social work* had emerged in the profession's vocabulary in the 1970s as a euphemism for *social casework, treatment-oriented social group work, social treatment, psychiatric social work,* and *direct practice* (Minahan, 1980, p. 171).

There are several implications of this changing vocabulary for the study of NASW members' characteristics and for any research on the nature of social work practice. To achieve an accurate description of where social workers work, what they do, and at what level of practice, NASW members must describe the same phenemona from the same perspective and with a common vocabulary. The popularity of Barker's (1992) *Social Work Dictionary* suggests that students and practitioners alike recognize the need for a common vocabulary.

To achieve a higher degree of accuracy among respondents to the annual survey may simply require the inclusion in the questionnaire of definitions of such terms as *practice setting, auspice,* and *function.* The repeated use of these terms in the social work literature to describe the same phenomena must be encouraged. For example, if *clinical practice* is the preferred term, then authors and editors must be required to use it, and *casework* and *psychiatric social work* must be dropped from the vocabulary and referred to only as historical terms.

In chapters 4 and 5, the obvious confusion about the differentiation between primary and secondary settings of practice and auspice and primary and secondary functions was discussed. But the lack of a standard vocabulary may be far more pervasive. For example, what, exactly, is management? The face validity of this and other terms used in social work surveys needs to be determined. Are NASW members describing the same phenomenon? Similarly, it should not be assumed that the meaning of *proprietary* and *for-profit services* is commonly understood.

Definitional issues affect the validity and reliability of any reports about the composition and nature of the work of the social work labor force. Steps must be taken to ensure that the vocabulary of the profession is standardized and understood by its members.

FUTURE DIRECTIONS

The trends that emerged from this study of the characteristics of NASW members suggest the following issues that the profession and NASW need to consider:

- The effectiveness of current strategies to recruit people of color and men.
- The characteristics of the clients served by social workers in different settings of practice and the implications for achieving the mission and goals of the profession.
- The differential use of social workers at the three educational levels—BSW, MSW, and PhD–DSW—for dealing with the more intractable social problems and at-risk clientele.
- How a more active public sector role can be reasserted.
- The means by which social work students and practitioners can be influenced to practice at the macro level.
- How the profession can achieve equity and parity in the salaries of men and women.

- How the profession can improve the preparation of practitioners for vertical and horizontal mobility in the profession, such as changes in functions and in practice settings.
- How the needs of practitioners for independence and self-actualization can be reconciled with the profession's role and mission to serve the most disadvantaged in society.

Questions about who social workers are would be clarified from the more extensive use of functional job analyses. We need to know more about the specific types of interventions that social workers use with what types of clients and in what settings. And, of course, continued emphasis on measuring the outcomes of social work intervention would yield essential information about the effectiveness of professional services.

REFERENCES

Abramovitz, M. (1986). The privatization of the welfare state: A review. *Social Work, 31,* 257–264.

Barker, R. L. (1984). *Social work in private practice: Principles, issues, and dilemmas.* Silver Spring, MD: National Association of Social Workers.

Barker, R. L. (1987). Private and proprietary services. In A. Minahan (Ed.-in-Chief), *Encyclopedia of social work* (18th ed., vol. 2, pp. 324–329). Silver Spring, MD: National Association of Social Workers.

Barker, R. L. (1992). *The social work dictionary* (2nd ed.). Washington, DC: National Association of Social Workers.

Battle, M. G. (1987). Professional associations: National Association of Social Workers. In A. Minahan (Ed.-in-Chief), *Encyclopedia of social work* (18th ed., vol. 2, pp. 333–341). Silver Spring, MD: National Association of Social Workers.

Beck, B. M. (1977). Professional associations: National Association of Social Workers. In J. B. Turner (Ed.-in-Chief), *Encyclopedia of social work* (17th ed., pp. 1084–1093). New York: National Association of Social Workers.

Becker, R. (1961). *Study of salaries of NASW members.* New York: National Association of Social Workers.

Bernard, L. D. (1987). Professional associations: Council on Social Work Education. In A. Minahan, (Ed.-in-Chief), *Encyclopedia of social work,* (18th ed., vol. 2, pp. 330–333). Silver Spring, MD: National Association of Social Workers.

Bureau of Labor Statistics. (1961). *Salaries and working conditions of social welfare manpower in 1960.* New York: National Social Welfare Assembly.

Bureau of Labor Statistics. (1991). *Household data survey: Employed civilians by detailed occupation, 1983–1991.* Washington, DC: Author.

Declassification. (1988). In *Social work speaks: NASW policy statements* (p. 155). Silver Spring, MD: National Association of Social Workers.

Etzioni, A. (Ed.). (1969). *The semi-professions and their organization.* New York: Free Press.

Gibelman, M. (1983). Social work education and public agency practice: Reassessing the partnership. *Journal of Social Work Education, 19*(3), 21–28.

Hopps, J. G., & Pinderhughes, E. B. (1987). Profession of Social Work: Contemporary characteristics. In A. Minahan (Ed.-in-Chief), *Encyclopedia of social work* (18th ed., vol. 2, pp. 351–366). Silver Spring, MD: National Association of Social Workers.

Jayaratne, S., Davis-Sacks, M. L., & Chess, W. (1991). Private practice may be good for your health. *Social Work, 36,* 224–232.

Minahan, A. (1980). What is clinical social work? (Editorial). *Social Work, 25,* 171.

Pecora, P. J., & Austin, M. J. (1983). Declassification of social service jobs: Issues and strategies. *Social Work, 28,* 421–426.

Saxton, P. M. (1988). Vendorship for social work: Observations on the maturation of the profession. *Social Work, 33,* 197–201.

Spaulding, E. (1991). *Statistics on social work education in the United States: 1990.* Alexandria, VA: Council on Social Work Education.

Staff. (1987). *Salaries in social work: A summary report on the salaries of NASW members, July 1986–June 1987.* Silver Spring, MD: National Association of Social Workers.

Walz, T., & Groze, V. (1991). The mission of social work revisited: An agenda for the 1990s. *Social Work, 36,* 500–504.

Williams, L. F. (1987). Professional associations: Special interest. In A. Minahan, (Ed.-in-Chief), *Encyclopedia of social work* (18th ed., pp. 341–346). Silver Spring, MD: National Association of Social Workers.

NASW MEMBERSHIP QUESTIONNAIRE

PERSONAL

Title First Name M.I. Last Name	Sex ☐F ☐M
Street	Date of Birth
Second Line Street Address	Home Phone #
City State Zip Code	Office Phone #

EMPLOYMENT

Title
Employer
Street
City   (Include Country, if foreign)   State   Zip Code

I would prefer to receive mailings at: Check one: ☐Home   ☐Office

There are NASW Chapters in all 50 states plus New York City, Metro Washington, D.C., Europe, Puerto Rico, and the Virgin Islands. PLEASE NOTE that you will be assigned a chapter based on your mailing preference address unless another chapter affiliation is requested here. *I would prefer to be assigned to the _____ chapter.

STUDENTS

Date entered current degree program: (Month and Year) _____/_____

Expected graduation date _____/_____

Anticipated degree (BSW, BS, MSW, ETC.)	College or University/Division/City & State	Major subject/ Program sequence

EDUCATION

Currently held degrees (List highest degree first)	Graduation Date Mo./Year	College or University/Division/ City & State	Major Subject/ Program sequence

ETHNIC ORIGIN

☐A. American Indian or Alaskan Native   ☐D. Chicano/Mexican American   ☐G. White (not Hispanic in Origin)
☐B. Asian or Pacific Islander   ☐E. Puerto Rican   ☐H. Other
☐C. Black (not Hispanic in Origin)   ☐F. Other Hispanic

Please check one ☐ new member ☐ former member (more than a year since renewing)

REGULAR MEMBERSHIP in NASW is open and limited to
anyone who has received an undergraduate or graduate degree
from a Council on Social Work Education (CSWE) accredited/
recognized program.

ASSOCIATE MEMBERSHIP is open and limited to anyone
currently employed full time in the U.S. in a social work capacity
(not self-employed or group private practice) who holds any accredited baccalaureate or greater degree, other than in social work.
Associate members are not eligible for liability insurance and may
not hold national office. However, national voting rights are extended
after 5 years of continuous membership.

RETIRED/UNEMPLOYED/DOCTORAL CANDIDATE
MEMBERSHIP. Reduced dues rates are available to regular
members who are retired or unemployed, i.e., totally unsalaried
in any field, or to degree candidates in social work doctoral
programs. In cases of temporary or extreme hardship, a reduction in
dues may be requested.

STUDENT MEMBERSHIP is open to anyone currently
enrolled in a Council on Social Work Education site-team
approved, accredited or recognized degree program.

| Prior Name (if previous member) |
| Prior I.D. No. |

Applicants who hold a degree from a foreign university should call the Membership Records Department
at the National Office for specific information on eligibility requirements.

METHOD OF PAYMENT—PLEASE CHECK ONE:

☐ Check or money order payable to NASW   ☐ VISA   ☐ MasterCard

Card No._____Exp. _____Amount $_____

AFFIRMATION

I hereby affirm and agree that I will abide by the Code of Ethics of the association and agree to submit to proceedings for any alleged violation of the same in accordance with NASW bylaws. I further understand that
falsification of the contents of this application will be grounds for rejection and/or termination of my association membership and revocation of any and all benefits resulting therefrom (see summary of code).

Signature_____ Date_____
CHECK, MONEY ORDER OR CHARGE CARD INFORMATION MUST ACCOMPANY THIS FORM.

Indicate your function in primary job and, if any, secondary job.

A. Direct Service (e.g., Casework, Group Work, Clinical)
B. Supervision
C. Management/Administration
D. Policy Development/Analysis
E. Consultant
F. Research
G. Planning
H. Education/Training
I. No Social Work Function

Primary _____   Secondary _____

Indicate auspice of your primary job and, if any, secondary job.

A. Public Service—Local
B. Public Service—State
C. Public Service—Federal
D. Public Service—Military
E. Private and Nonprofit—Secretarian
F. Private and Nonprofit—Non-Sectarian
G. Private for Profit; Proprietary

Primary _____   Secondary _____

Indicate setting of primary job and, if any, secondary job.

A. Social Service Agency/Organization
B. Private Practice—Self-Employed/Solo
C. Private Practice—Partnership/Group
D. Membership Organization
E. Hospital
F. Institution (Non-Hospital)
G. Outpatient Facility: Clinic/ Health or Mental Health Ctr.
H. Group Home/Residence
I. Nursing Home/Hospice
J. Court/Criminal Justice System
K. College/University
L. Elementary/Secondary School System
M. Employment in Non-Social Service Organization (e.g., business/manufacturing; consulting/research firm; etc.)

Primary _____   Secondary _____

Indicate practice area of primary job and, if any, secondary job.

A. Children & Youth
B. Community Organizing/Planning
C. Family Services
D. Correction/Criminal Justice
E. Group Services
G. Mental Health
H. Public assistance/Welfare
I. School Social Work
J. Services to Aged
K. Alcohol/Drug & Substance Abuse
L. Developmental Disability/Mental Retardation
N. Occupational
O. Other (specify) _____

Primary _____   Secondary _____

Indicate the first and second practice commission with which you identify.*

A. Health/Mental Health Commission (e.g., Medical/Health Care, Mental Health, Disabilities, etc.)

B. Family and Primary Associations Commission (e.g., Children and Youth, Family Services, Services to the Aged, etc.)

C. Education commission (e.g., Social "Work in Schools, Colleges, etc.)"

D. Employment/Economic Support Commission (e.g., Occupational Social Work, Assistance/Public Welfare, etc.)

E. Justice Commission (e.g., Corrections, Criminal Justice, etc.)

*NOTE: In 1985 NASW identified 5 fields of practice and established "5 Commissions" as an initial organizing framework for response to member's practice interests. The Justice Commission is not currently operational.

First _____   Second _____

Indicate current annual salary (or self-employed income) from primary employment only

- [ ] A. Under $10,000
- [ ] B. $10,000-14,999
- [ ] C. $15,000-17,499
- [ ] D. $17,500-19,999
- [ ] E. $20,000-24,999
- [ ] F. $25,000-29,999
- [ ] G. $30,000-34,999
- [ ] H. $35,000-39,999
- [ ] I. $40,000-49,999
- [ ] J. $50,000-59,999
- [ ] K. $60,000-69,999
- [ ] L. $70,000-79,999
- [ ] M. $80,000 & Over

The annual salary reported above is for:

- [ ] Full-time
- [ ] Part-time

Indicate annual income from secondary employment, if any:

- [ ] A. Under $2,500
- [ ] B. $2,500-4,999
- [ ] C. $5,000-9,999
- [ ] D. $10,000-14,999
- [ ] E. $15,000-19,999
- [ ] F. $20,000 & Over

Indicate total years of social work experience since first social work degree:

- [ ] A. Under 2 years
- [ ] B. 2-5 years
- [ ] C. 6-10 years
- [ ] D. 11-15 years
- [ ] E. 16-20 years
- [ ] F. 21-25 years
- [ ] G. Over 25 years

INDEX

—

A

Academy of Certified Social Workers
(ACSW), 11, 16
active membership status in, 33
1988–90 study conducted by, 12–13
Validation Study of 1983–84, 12
African American members
employed
by experience, 44, 45
by gender, 36, 38
total, 42
in primary auspice, 59–62, 75
primary function of, 94–97
primary income of, 111, 112
primary practice area of, 82–85, 88–90
in primary settings, 68, 70–72
secondary function of, 100
in secondary settings, 73, 74
total, 20–21
African Americans in social work
positions, 131
Age
of employed members
by gender, 38–40
by social work degrees, 41–42
by primary income, 111, 113, 114
by primary practice area, 83, 86, 87
total members, 23–24, 130–131
American Association for Marriage and
Family Therapy, 132
American Public Welfare Association, 132
Asian members
employed, 38, 43
by experience, 44, 45
by gender, 38
total, 43

in primary auspice, 59–62
primary function of, 94–97
primary income of, 111, 112
primary practice area of, 82–85, 89–90
in primary settings, 68, 70, 72
secondary function of, 100
in secondary settings, 74
total, 21
Auspice. *See* Primary auspice; Secondary
auspice

B

Barker, R. L., 135
Becker, R., 12
Bureau of Labor Statistics (BLS)
estimates of social work labor force in
1991, 4, 19, 20, 131
*Household Data Survey: Employed
Civilians by Detailed Occupation,
1983–1991,* 12
1961 study on social welfare personnel,
12
use of data from, 2

C

Casework, 16, 138, 139
Chicano members. *See also* Hispanic
members
employed
by experience, 44
by gender, 36, 38
by social work degree, 44
total, 42–43
in primary auspice, 59–62
primary function of, 94, 96, 97
primary income of, 111, 112

147

THE AUTHORS

Margaret Gibelman, DSW, ACSW, is visiting associate professor, The Catholic University of America, National Catholic School of Social Service, Washington, DC. She has worked in the human services as a clinician, supervisor, educator, and manager. In the latter category, she has served as executive director, National Association of School Psychologists and, earlier, the Lupus Foundation of America. She was also associate executive director, Council on Social Work Education.

Dr. Gibelman frequently consults with nonprofit organizations and is the author of numerous articles on nonprofit management, privatization, mediation and negotiation, continuing education, health care policy and financing, and service delivery systems.

Philip H. Schervish, PhD, is assistant professor, The Catholic University of America, National Catholic School of Social Service, Washington, DC. He has practiced social work as manager, supervisor, direct service practitioner, and instructor since 1971. He received an MPA and a PhD in social work. After serving six years as legislative analyst and program evaluator for the Indiana General Assembly, he taught at Indiana University School of Social Work.

His past research includes a national study of just compensation, models for redefining poverty in the United States, and studies of information use by social workers in mental health settings. He has assisted with the development of university-based social work curricula in the former Soviet Union. His current research interests focus around information technology applications for decision support in policy and practice, social justice in social welfare policy, and development of the social work profession.

To Help You Publish

FROM NASW PRESS . . .

Who We Are: The Social Work Labor Force as Reflected in the NASW Membership
by Margaret Gibelman and Philip Schervish

This book uses the membership base of NASW—the world's largest organization of professional social workers—to provide a look at the social work labor force and how it has changed over time. Chapters present demographic information, examine and compare social work salaries, and shed light on which fields of practice, work settings, and job functions attract social workers most. The authors also examine labor force trends for their effects on the future of the profession. **$24.95**

Social Work Almanac
by Leon Ginsberg

The most comprehensive compilation of statistical social welfare data available in one source. Provides clear, succinct information on virtually every human services category. Entries include basic demography, income, children, crime and delinquency, education, health, mental health, older adults, social welfare issues, and the social work profession. **$29.95**

Professional Writing for the Human Services
edited by Linda Beebe

Learn basic writing techniques, how to conduct a literature search, how to write qualitative and quantitative research reports, and how to present statistical data graphically. Delve into the mysteries of the peer review process and discover how to package your journal article or book proposal to best advantage. NASW's own style and citation guides plus references for production techniques, ethical issues, copyright concerns, and more make this the most comprehensive writing guide available for the human services. An excellent resource for all forms of professional writing. **$26.95**

An Author's Guide to Social Work Journals, Third Edition
by Henry N. Mendelsohn

Helps authors find the right journal for their manuscript. Provides detailed publishing requirements and guidelines for over 130 human services journals plus a selected bibliography on style and writing guides. **$24.95**

Save 10% with the NASW Writer's Special . . . a collection of new publications designed to help you research, write, and find the appropriate publisher for your work.

Human services writers from the neophyte to the experienced author can prepare their writing and research for publication with the valued reference books featured in NASW's **Writer's Special.** For years, writers have depended on NASW for the information they need to publish in the human services. Now, for the low price of $73.65, you can receive three of NASW's top reference books for writers—**Social Work Almanac;** the widely used and useful **Author's Guide to Social Work Journals,** in its new third edition; and **Professional Writing for the Human Services.**

Save even more when you buy **Who We Are** *and the NASW Writer's Special together!*

Order the NASW **Writer's Special** and get **Who We Are** at a 15% savings! You'll get the classic reference collection that includes the two-volume **Encyclopedia of Social Work** (18th edition), the **1990 Encyclopedia of Social Work Supplement,** and the 2nd edition of **The Social Work Dictionary**—and you'll receive **Who We Are** at the special price of $21.20.

To order, see the form on the reverse side of this card.

ORDER FORM

☐ Send me the NASW Press publications checked below.

Title	Item #	Price	Total
☐ Who We Are	Item #2251	$24.95	
☐ Social Work Almanac	Item #1964	$29.95	
☐ Professional Writing for the Human Services	Item #1999	$26.95	
☐ An Author's Guide to Social Work Journals	Item #2197	$24.95	
☐ NASW Writer's Special	Item #A15	$73.65	
☐ Who We Are/NASW Writer's Special Package	Item #P90	$94.85	
	+ 10% postage and handling		
	Total		

☐ I've enclosed my check or money order for $_____.

☐ Please charge my credit card. ☐ NASW Visa ☐ Other Visa ☐ MasterCard

Credit Card No. _____ Exp. Date _____

Signature _____

Name _____

Address _____

City _____ State _____ Zip _____

(Payment must accompany this order. Make checks payable to NASW Press.)

Send to—

NASW Distribution Center
P.O. Box 431
Annapolis JCT, MD 20701

Call toll free—

1-800-227-3590
(in Metro DC area, 301-604-6664)

Or fax—
301-206-7989